THE GREAT EXCHANGE

Why Your Prayer Requests May Not Be Getting Answers

P. Douglas Small

The Great Exchange
Why Your Prayer Requests May Not Be Getting Answers

ISBN: 978-0-9896525-8-2

Published by Alive Publications
a division of
Alive Ministries: PROJECT PRAY
PO Box 1245
Kannapolis, NC 28082

www.alivepublications.org

www.projectpray.org

Consider *Why Your Prayer Requests May Not Be Getting Answers - The Great Exchange* companion Personal and Group Study Guide. *The Great Exchange* Resource Kit is even more complete with Teaching Guide, PowerPoint and videos tied to the book and teaching guide. Available at www.alivepublications.org.

*To my five children – Phyllis Michelle, Helena Cheryl,
Dalena Rechelle, Phillip Michael and Alycia LouAnn –
all followers of Jesus Christ!*

*To the memory of the times the children prayed,
sang or led family worship.*

*To night-time, bedside prayers – so sweet and innocent.
A bag of gold would be small change, a meager price, were
it to grant a trip back in time to experience
such precious moments again.*

Cover artwork created by Brendon Farley.

Table of Contents

Foreword

When I think of Doug Small, I think of prayer. I first met him years ago at a prayer conference. When I came to Holmes Bible College, he was a member of the Board of Trustees, and through the years he has always been focused on prayer.

The Great Exchange is a powerful book on prayer. Anyone interested in developing an effective prayer life individually or corporately needs to read this book. It is very practical, for Doug writes out of his vast experience in studying prayer and teaching prayer in numerous conferences. As you read this book, you will see many steps to a more consistent life of prayer. I intend to use the book in my Spiritual Formation class to provide our students with a practical guide for a victorious prayer life.

The Great Exchange is grounded in the Word. Doug gives an exposition of Philippians 4:4-7 as the scriptural basis for the study. The heart of the passage is *"By prayer and supplication, with thanksgiving, let your request be known to God...."* We bring to God our anxieties, our stress, our needs in prayer and God answers our prayers by giving to us His blessings of peace and protection. There is a powerful exchange that takes place in prayer. The idea of the "exchanged life" is a fresh and innovative concept on the power of prayer.

The book is a great read. It is filled with great illustrations which will encourage the reader. It also has numerous quotes from men and women of prayer which give testimony of the power of prayer to bring about a wonderful exchange in our lives.

Doug Small is an outstanding leader in the prayer movement in this country and internationally. The focus of his ministry is prayer. He is president of Alive Ministries: PROJECT PRAY which is dedicated to increasing the prayer life of individuals and of churches. He often speaks of creating a praying church. He is the prayer director of his denomination, Church of God, Cleveland, TN. He is involved in a number of international prayer initiatives. His contribution to the prayer movement is immeasurable.

Doug is a dynamic speaker as well as a gifted writer on prayer. He has spoken at the college on more than one occasion, and his presentations have been amazing. The faculty, staff and students are greatly blessed by his teaching and preaching. He is one of our favorite speakers. He is an outstanding communicator of spiritual and scriptural truth. He makes you want to live a more committed prayer life.

The Great Exchange will be an invaluable book for individual study or for a Bible study for groups. Every person serious about prayer needs a copy of this book.

Bishop James D. Leggett
President of Holmes Bible College

Preface

After the book was finished, I re-read it, and reflected on its call to a buoyant life of joy and peace in the midst of personal pain. I also found myself in a baptism of lament psalms.

So, as a matter of balance – let's say, God wants us to live in victory. We are to live out of the resurrection. Three times in the ministry of Jesus, he met death with resurrection. He put away the tears of the family of Jarius and the widow of Nain, and raised their children from the dead. And yet, at the tomb of Lazarus, he too wept. So, it's okay to weep. The goal is this book is not to produce plastic Christians who are superficially 'happy,' but to suggest a deeper level of joy and peace, in the middle of any life crisis – and that by grace.

One theologian reduced prayer to two positions – petition or praise. His thesis, drawn from the psalms, was simple. Need moves us to petition. It distracts. It drains. It saps our joy and disturbs our peace. So, the Psalms declares, *"I will praise thee: for thou hast heard me, and art become my salvation"* (118:21). Because you have answered me, I will praise you.

Living out of the resurrection, there is a higher standard, namely, I will praise you before you answer. And as I make my petition, I will do so in joy and peace. And if there is no answer or one different than my request – I will praise you still.

This is Paul's thesis in Philippians: *"Rejoice in the Lord, always… Let the peace of God guard you heart and mind."* It's unrealistic. Who lives here? Peace in the storm. Joy in disappointment. We should say, for balance, it is okay to be human. In fact, the Bible gives us permission to lament, to weep in the face of disappoint and to complain to God. That we keep praying is evidence of faith – even if it is little faith like a mustard seed, even if it is 'I believe, help my unbelief' – that we keep praying and hoping, is progress.

In reading this book, I pray that you will discover a key to tapping grace even before God lifts your burden and answers your prayer. I pray that you will learn to make 'the great exchange,' your burdens for His victory.

I Must Tell Jesus

I must tell Jesus all of my trials,
I cannot bear these burdens alone;
In my distress He kindly will help me,
He ever loves and cares for His own.

Refrain:
I must tell Jesus! I must tell Jesus!
I cannot bear my burdens alone;
I must tell Jesus! I must tell Jesus!
Jesus can help me, Jesus alone.

I must tell Jesus all of my troubles,
He is a kind, compassionate Friend;
If I but ask Him He will deliver,
Make of my troubles quickly an end.

Tempted and tried I need a great Savior,
One who can help my burdens to bear;
I must tell Jesus, I must tell Jesus:
He all my cares and sorrows will share.

What must I do when worldliness calls me?
What must I do when tempted to sin?
I must tell Jesus, and He will help me
Over the world the vict'ry to win.[1]

CHAPTER ONE
Answers to Prayer

Perspective: The lack of answers to our prayers is not because God no longer answers or does not want to help. It is often an issue on our side – some hindrance to prayer, blockages in our own heart. In such moments, no one is more disappointed than God. He wants to help us, to deliver, to answer. Prayer works, because God works. It is effective, because its hope is in Him and His action. But it also demands changes in us. There are prerequisites to answered prayer. Often, what we call difficulty in prayer is our resistance to meeting the conditions necessary to prevail in prayer; and yet, prayer is never a matter of mechanics – step one, two, three; or of our perfect execution in faith or example, it is always by grace. Still, there is a transformational component to prayer, as there is a transactional element. God uses prayer to change us; and he uses prayer to change things. But often the great change is not in things external, alone, but in us. Prayer can never be seen as merely transactional – a mere exchange of information or requisitions and orders for fulfillment between heaven and earth. God has transformation in mind.

Introduction

Elisha Hoffman was a pastor and the son of a pastor. He was a pastor, serving the Benton Harbor Presbyterian Church for more than three decades. His pastime was writing hymns. One day, in the midst of his pastoral duties, in a sea of destitute people, he met among them a woman whose depression seemed permanent. As she poured out her heart to the pastor, it was clear that her situation was beyond mere human help. "What shall I do? O, what shall I do?" she frantically asked. Pastor Hoffman knew that he could not step under such a load. He had no answer, but God did. "You cannot do better than to take all your sorrows to Jesus. *You must tell Jesus,*" he urged. Her face lit up.

"Yes," she cried. "That's it! *I must tell Jesus.*" When Hoffman returned to his study, the resolute word he had given the woman; words she had echoed, rang in his soul. He sat down and penned the great hymn, *"I must tell Jesus! I cannot bear my burdens alone…Jesus can help me, Jesus alone."*[2]

God Making

In our day Christians turn to others – pastors, counselors, friends and family – and ask them to do what only God can do. Out of empathy, we sometimes assume the burdens of loved ones, and naively attempt to solve problems that can only be managed by God. We offer well-meaning mercy that distracts others from a greater depth of prayer and persistent dependence on God. Imperceptibly, we present ourselves as more compassionate than God. Others, looking to us and coming to depend on us, unwittingly "god-make" us, asking us to help them, and we, under the banner of nobility, assume that role. It feels good to be made a god – but the result is a train wreck, multiplied heartache and unhealthy co-dependent social patterns.

We are certainly suppose to bear one another's burdens, to pray for one another, to be people of compassion. Yet, no one can do our praying for us – and codependent dynamics that substitute for primary dependence on God are counterproductive to spiritual maturity. Prayer is first telling Jesus – not others! At least, not before we tell God. And though we have the glorious privilege of asking things of God, petition (prayer requests) are not the center of prayer. They must be understood inside a larger picture of prayer. Heartfelt, worshipful communion with God must be the anchor of prayer. We can ask God for things only because we *abide* in him (John 15:7). The strength of our asking is rooted in the depth and quality of our worshipful relationship. We offer our needs in humble dependence and faith in God's *character*, not simply his *ability*. Petition is more than a matter of acquisition. It is evidence of our confidence in God's love and care for us. Intercession (prayer for others) reveals our lack of selfishness as we plea to God for others and their needs. All of these – communion, petition and intercession – are wrapped in gratitude, trumpeted by our open thanksgiving. It is our thanksgiving that validates the vitality of our faith; it opens the gate toward His presence (Psalm 100:4), it buoys faith when needs press in around us; it reminds us that God acted in the past, and He will do so again.

God Answers Prayer

From Genesis to Revelation, the God of the Bible answers prayer. And that is quite extraordinary – an accessible God, a caring God, an action God, a responsive and loving God. Survey the religions of the world and you find this God to be utterly unique. But answers to prayer are not a panacea. God received Abel's worshipful sacrifice and to him God was favorable. In that sense, He answered Abel's prayer, but Cain, his brother, refused to meet the conditions of the altar. He insisted on coming to God in his own way and God did not receive Cain's sacrifice. He could not retaliate against God, so being full of rage; he murdered Abel (Genesis 4:8). God answered Elijah's prayer and the fire fell on Mt. Carmel. When Ahab went home from church that morning and told his wife Jezebel what had happened, she put a price on Elijah's head and issued an all-points bulletin for his arrest. Elijah's prayer was answered, but his life endangered in the same movement (I Kings 19:1-3). An angel came to strengthen Jesus as He prayed in the garden, but He was still headed for the cross (Luke 22:43).

We tend to see prayer as an exit route from trouble, as an escape. At times, God does open a Red Sea (Exodus 14:21), cool a furnace (Daniel 3:25), shut the mouths of lions (Daniel 6:20-22), heal the bite of a viper (Acts 28:3-6) and raise the dead (Acts 20:8-10). But prayer is more than mere magic. Sometimes prayer is the fountain from which miracles seem to flow. But mostly, it is the mysterious means by which we are allowed to be partners with God in ways we will not completely understand until we arrive on heaven's shores.

Examples of Answered Prayer

A Canadian minister confessed, "I am frequently impressed by the Spirit to perform actions...These impressions are so vivid that I dare not disobey them." These impressions to pray, at times, result in remarkable interventions. In this case, on a stormy night, the minister was impressed to go some distance to the home of an aged couple and pray. The impression was compelling. He arrived finding a door open. He entered the house, seeing no one, and knelt in fervent prayer. "I poured out my petitions to God, in an audible voice, for divine protection..." Finishing prayer, he simply returned home. Months later, while visiting a prison, he was confronted by an agitated inmate who claimed to know him. "Do you remember going to a house one night and offering prayer?" He recalled the strange occasion, and asked the prisoner how he came to know about it. The inmate confessed that he "had gone to that house to steal a sum of money, known to be in the possession of the old man." He was waiting when the minister arrived, and at first, he thought it was the old man returning, "When you drove into the yard, I thought you were he, and intended to kill you...I followed you into the house, and heard your prayer. You prayed for God to protect the old people from violence of any kind and especially from murder; and if there was any hand uplifted to strike them, that it ought to be paralyzed." Then the prisoner pointed to his right arm, hanging lifeless by his side, "Do you see that arm? It was paralyzed on the spot, and I have never moved it since."[3]

Hudson Taylor was the founder of China Inland Mission. His father was so consumed with the spiritual need of China that he covenanted with God for a son that might labor as a missionary to that land. It was not until Hudson had served seven years that he knew that story. At the age of 15, he was still a skeptic. While away on a trip, his mother rose from the dinner table with an intense yearning for his conversion. She locked herself into her bedroom, and pleaded with God, resolving not to leave the room until her prayers were answered. Hours passed. Finally, all she could do was praise God for Hudson's conversion. Hudson recalled, "A light was flashed into my soul by the Holy Spirit that there was nothing to be done, but to fall on my knees and accept this Savior and His salvation, and praise God forevermore." While his mother was on her knees praising God in her closet, he was meeting Christ in an old warehouse miles away. When he returned home, his mother met him with a knowing confidence, "I know, my boy; I have been rejoicing for a fortnight in the glad tidings you have to tell me!"[4]

John Wesley had been laboring in the Norman Islands. Dr. Adam Clark, the great preacher and commentator, was among those who boarded an English brig and left for Bristol with a fine, fair breeze, expecting a quick passage. Soon, they were met with a rather fierce contrary wind. Wesley was in his cabin reading. Hearing the bustle on deck, he inquired about the cause and discovering the difficulty, he urged, "Let us go to prayer." Each man prayed, and then

Wesley broke out into fervent supplication. Clark would comment on how unusual it seemed, "More the offspring of strong faith than mere desire," he discerned. Wesley prayed,

> Almighty and everlasting God, you have your say everywhere, and all things serve the purposes of your will. *You hold the winds in your fists,* and upon the water floods, and you reign a king forever. Command these winds and these waves, that they obey Thee, and take us speedily and safely to the haven where we would be.

Wesley rose from his knees, made no remark, but simply picked up his book and continued reading. Dr. Clark went on deck. To his surprise, he found the vessel back on course aided by a steady breeze that did not abate until they reached harbor. Wesley never commented on the remarkable turn of the weather. "So fully," says Dr. Clark, "did he expect to be heard, that he took it for granted he was heard." He received and expected regular answers to prayer – "therefore to him the occurrence was not strange."[5]

Hindrances to Prayer

D. L. Moody once said, "Next to the wonder of seeing my Savior will be, I think, the wonder that I made so little use of the power of prayer." Dr. John R. Rice often spoke of the hindrances to prayer. Below is a list of seven.

1. Personal sin in the believer's life.
2. Strained known relationships between husbands and wives.
3. Wrongs, debts, or offenses not reconciled between Christian brothers and sisters.
4. An unforgiving or bitter spirit.
5. The sin of covetousness.
6. Neglect and indifference to the Word of God.
7. Prayerlessness itself.

William Cowper, the great poet and lyricist penned the lines, "What various hindrances we meet; in coming to the mercy-seat."[6] Sadly, most hindrances are of our own making. Someone declared,

> God wants me to pray. The devil does not want me to pray, and does all he can to hinder me. He knows that we can accomplish more through our prayers than through our work. He would rather have us do anything else than pray.[7]

Heart Blockages

The problem in prayer is not the unwillingness of Christ to hear. It is often some "little sin" that damages and spoils our prayer life. In addition to those above, there are other hindrances that block our access to grace.

1. Doubt and Unbelief
2. Self
3. Having a judgmental attitude
4. Unresolved Inner Conflict
5. A Love Deficit
6. An Angry Disposition
7. Always Praying Alone
8. The Lack of Thanksgiving and Praise
9. Heart Idols
10. Lack of Compassion for the Poor

All these can be resolved if only we will repent, be broken and transparent before God. Humility is the gateway to purity. The problem is rarely the depth of the sin's stain on the heart, but the hardness of the heart itself.

'Golden Rule Jones' served as the Mayor of Toledo, Ohio during the Great Depression. He sometimes doubled as a presiding judge in the city's night court. One night a man charged with stealing was before the bench. His defense was that his family was hungry. He was out of work, a victim of hard times, and desperate. The judge reprimanded him. "You did not steal from society…you stole from a private citizen, and you broke the law. I am fining you ten dollars." Then he reached inside his pocket and paid the fine for the defendant. He then charged everyone in the courtroom of being guilty of living in a city that made it necessary for a man to steal to provide for his family. Passing a hat around, he instructed everyone to put in 50 cents and gave the proceeds to the defendant.[8] Justice satisfies the law, and mercy pays the fine. Grace, driven by compassion, adds a blessing. Grace does not dismantle righteousness, but mercy understands that the law was made for the man, not man for the law.

REVIEW It

1. Review the seven classic reasons prayer is hindered and unanswered.

2. "Most _____ to prayer are of our own making!" Agree or disagree?

3. What is the difference between _____ and judging? Is there a difference?

4. Inner _____, a polluted sanctuary of the heart, is a heart-stopping blockage to prayer.

5. Had you ever seen the idea of our lack of _____ for the poor and needy as a hindrance to prayer? Do you care for the needy? Does your church? In what practical way?

TALK About It

1. Of the stories to answered prayer in this chapter, which is your favorite? Tell why? God is seen as saving, protecting, providing, sending angels, and controlling winds in relationship with prayer – How do we understand such things? Share your own story of answered prayer.

2. Of the ten heart-blockages, which ones do you think we struggle with the most? Which one do you struggle with the most? What are your plan for overcoming?

3. Rank the heart-blockages, all ten, from "my greatest chance of a spiritual heart-attack" to the least. (See Rating Sheet in Appendix.) Make them a matter of prayer.

4. Talk about the need for spiritual heart-health as a prerequisite for effective praying.

5. Do you think our culture has accepted a double standard – "in *private* anything goes," all is right, and that is not a matter for *public* consideration in terms of qualification for political office or perhaps even spiritual leadership? What are the dangers of such a view? How do we respond? What would Jesus have said?

Endnotes

1. Elisha A. Hoffman, *I Must Tell Jesus* (Lyrics: Copyright: Public Domain, 1893).

2. Robert J. Morgan, *More Real Stories for the Soul* (Nashville, TN: Thomas Nelson Publishers, 2000), 4-5.

3. Ibid, Story by Lily Blake Blakeney Howe, "A Would-Be Murderer's Arm Paralyzed," 21.

4. S. B. Shaw, *Touching Incidents And Remarkable Answers To Prayer* (Grand Rapids, MI: S. B. Shaw, Publisher, 1893), 33.

5. Ibid, 128.

6. William Cowper, *Olney Hymns* (London: W. Oliver, 1779), Number 60.

7. Author Unknown, *The Kneeling Christian* (Kessinger Publishing, 2004), Chapter 11: "Hindrances to Prayer."

8. Bruce Larson, *The Presence: The God Who Delivers and Guides* (HarperCollins Publishers, 1988), 132.

REVIEW It Answers

1. Personal Known Sin; Strained Relationships; Wrongs Not Reconciled; Unforgiveness; Covetousness; Neglect of Scripture; Prayerlessness itself
2. Hindrances
3. Discerning
4. Heart-idols
5. Compassion

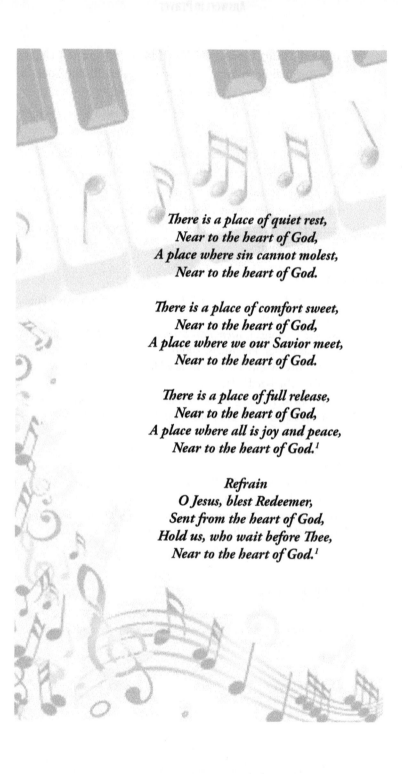

There is a place of quiet rest,
Near to the heart of God,
A place where sin cannot molest,
Near to the heart of God.

There is a place of comfort sweet,
Near to the heart of God,
A place where we our Savior meet,
Near to the heart of God.

There is a place of full release,
Near to the heart of God,
A place where all is joy and peace,
Near to the heart of God.[1]

Refrain
O Jesus, blest Redeemer,
Sent from the heart of God,
Hold us, who wait before Thee,
Near to the heart of God.[1]

CHAPTER TWO
Getting Started

Perspective: Nothing will jump-start the prayer life of a believer and launch them further and faster, than creating a place of prayer – it is the intentionality of it that is so important. It translates an idea into a real place, and a place begs for a time. So determine to meet God there regularly, daily, if possible. Next, develop a prayer regimen. Bring some structure to your experience of prayer. Create your own prayer pattern and list. Don't become legalistic about it, but use it as a gentle guide to keep yourself focused. Expand prayer beyond your narrow slice of pain.

Two things tower over all others in grounding a regular prayer habit – and they are a *place* and *time* to pray!

Creating a Place to Pray

If possible, create a dedicated prayer room. Jesus said, *"But you, when you pray, go into your inner room, close your door and pray to your Father who is in secret, and your Father who sees what is done in secret will reward you"* (Matthew 6:6 NASB). The "inner room" is also translated "inner chamber" or "closet" – thus the term "prayer closet." Devoted Jews in the time of Christ often had a special place for prayer, sometimes a small room on the edge of their rooftop. Creating a dedicated space for prayer – a room, a closet, a corner – will advance your prayer life by lightyears. Stock it with different translations of the Bible, a notepad, prayer helps and reminders, maps for missionary and city praying, devotional prayer guides, and even newspaper clippings worthy of your prayer notice. (Prayer should be relevant; it is the space where eternity touches time and God's will intersects with our world.)

Choose a place away from distractions, a place with some level of privacy. It should be large enough to allow you to get on your knees, and at times on your face. Don't take the telephone with you. Being able to "shut a door" is the ability to disconnect from this world, and travel to another, "shutting yourself in" to God. Ringing phones and doorbells have an uncanny sense of timing – as if intended by some malevolent force to distract.

Setting a Time to Pray

Determine, if at all possible, to *pray every day* – at or near the same time. Don't be legalistic, but do be disciplined. The same time might be "the first thing you do" in the morning. It might be the first or last thing you do each evening. The late David Wilkerson set aside an evening time for prayer, during which God directed him to the streets of New York and launched him into a global ministry.

Luther, the great Reformer, confessed, "If I fail to spend two hours in prayer each morning, the devil gets the victory through the day. I have so much business I cannot get on without spending three hours daily in prayer."[2] He prayed in the morning and the more pressing his day, the more time he devoted to prayer. Someone has said, "Prayer is not," as we suppose, "a time *taker*. It is a time *maker.*" Prayer invites God to work in our work – and that shortens the work process. Otherwise, we struggle alone.

Charles Simeon devoted the hours from four till eight in the

morning to God. John Wesley, the founder of the Methodist movement, spent two hours daily in prayer, beginning at four in the morning. And at the top of every hour, Wesley disciplined himself to turn
his heart toward heaven, and pray for some five minutes, even when
he was on the back of a horse traveling to another preaching station.
Above all else, prayer was his business. A friend declared, "I have seen
him come out of his closet with a serenity of face next to shining."[3]

Great men of God prayed – regularly, daily, and consistently.
Such examples are intimidating to us, so relax. Just begin, with all
sincerity, to attempt to meet with God daily. When you miss a day,
don't grovel in guilt. God is not nearly so disappointed *with* you
when you miss your daily appointment with Him, as He is disappointed *for* you. Prayer is the context in which He whispers secrets,
dispenses blessings, determines to meet us openly in the course of the
day since we determined to meet Him privately.

These two things – a *place* for prayer, and a regular *time* for prayer
are cornerstones in beginning a prayer life. Treat your daily *appointment* with God as non-optional. Mandatory. Irrevocable. Who else
could you meet with that is more important than God?

What to Do In Your Prayer Room

- READ SCRIPTURE. The Bible is our prayer book. Good
  prayer is always over an open Bible. There is no true prayer
  apart from it.
- REHEARSE GOD'S GOODNESS. Begin prayer time with
  a review of the goodness of God during the past 24 hours.
  Rehearse moments in which you saw traces of His hand. Give
  thanks. Refuse to take food, shelter and safety for granted.
- COMMUNE WITH GOD. Spend time in communion with
  God. Let Him talk to you out of Scripture. Center yourself in
  His love. This is the heart of prayer. Don't rush.
- PRESENT YOUR NEEDS. Move from communion with

God to petition – present your needs to God. Detail them. Tell God your problems as if He were uninformed about your situation. Stake your claim on the basis of Scripture.

- PRAISE. Partner your petitions with praise. Get your eyes off the problem. Fixating on giants only causes you to feel like a grasshopper (Numbers 13:33).
- INTERCEDE. Pray for others. Petition is presenting your needs to God. Intercession is petitioning for others. In intercession, you pray as if you were the other person.
- PRAY SPECIFICALLY. Make a list of those for whom you need to pray – family, friends, Christian workers, missionaries, civic and political leaders, outstanding sinners, the weak and oppressed, and bold Christians who are on the front lines. Make a list of people for whom you care that don't have a relationship with Christ. Write their names down – call them out daily. Adopt a nation, other than your own, for daily prayer.
- PRAY ALOUD. Meditation is a valid form of prayer – but meditation is not the same as praying. Prayer demands words. And spoken prayer demands that rambling thoughts be organized and offered to God in a coherent way. Meditation and prayer are partners.
- LISTEN. Expect to hear from God. Wait on the Lord. Keep a note pad handy, or a journal. Powerful inspirations come during prayer. Make notes of your encounters with God.
- PRAY EARLY. Praying in the morning will serve to create an atmosphere of prayer throughout the day. You will find yourself snatching otherwise latent and empty time frames and filling them with prayer.

Creating Your Prayer List[4]

- Pray for **Christian character.**
- Pray **that you do *no* evil,** that your behavioral choices will honor our Father.

- Pray **that your love may abound** toward all people.
- Pray for **the unsaved,** the harvest.
- Pray for **grace toward others** – especially those to whom you need to extend forgiveness.
- Pray **that God will open doors** for the ministry of the Word.
- Pray **for the peace of Jerusalem.**
- Pray for **national and local leaders of government.**

Additional Helpful Prayer Tips[5]

1. **Develop a Plan.** Don't be overwhelmed. Start slow. Keep things simple at the beginning. Most people get discouraged in prayer because their prayer time has no or little structure. Without a plan, you drift.

2. **Pray without ceasing.** Praying in the morning in a less than casual way is a doorway to living in an attitude of prayer. Having a *time* and a *place,* and a *prayer plan* are tethers for a life lived with the wind of the Spirit driving our sails.

3. **Just Talk to God!** Prayer doesn't require the use of 'thee' and 'thous' – nor does it forbid it. However, neither the terms in your vocabulary nor volume or tone of your voice need to change. It might, but even when passion comes to prayer, you should still be you – natural. Naturally spiritual.

4. **Take Notes.** Expect assignments from God. Without a record of God-encounters, it is too easy to forget moments you have had – answers, impressions, words and promises.

5. **Pray about Everything.** And keep it simple. In the days of Jesus, the Jewish believers had standard prayers for everything – plowing a field, eating a meal, drinking, a wedding, a funeral – everything.

6. **Keep Prayer Happy and Holy.** *"Rejoice in the Lord, always. Again I say, rejoice!"* is the prelude to presenting needs, pulsating painful needs. They must not so overwhelm us to take away our joy. Happy, yet holy.

7. **Pray for Provision.** Jesus taught us to pray for our *"daily bread."*

8. **Pray for Protection**. Never take God's protective care for granted. *"Because he has given me his love, I will take him out of danger: I will put him in a place of honor, because he has kept my name in his heart"* (Psalms 91:14 BBE).

9. **Pray for Direction**. Ask God to order your steps. Give God glory! Our whole purpose for being on the earth is to give God glory. Remember – *Anybody Can Pray!*

10. **Partner Praise and Thanksgiving with Prayer.** Every need is to be presented with the recollection of God's actions of grace in the past; every appeal for God's intervention is paired with praise that affirms God's ability and character. We enter God's presence with thanksgiving and we exit in praise.

In his book, *The Purple Pig*, Dick Eastman tells the story of Benny, a 15-year-old teen with the mind of a six year old. The evening, dedicated to an opportunity for young people to share how God was at work in their lives, was spontaneous and unpredictable. Such unfiltered times are often fresh with sincere unpolished God stories. Four kids stood ready to share. Benny too decided he had something on his heart that compelled him forward. There were a few giggles, anticipating a train wreck, but Benny was not giggling. His eyes brimmed with tears; they stained his face. His lips were quivering.

"I know what you are thinking," the husky 15-year-old mumbled. "Benny is going to ruin everything. He's gonna wreck this whole meeting. He can't even give a good testimony…I know I am not normal. I'm not like all of you. I was born different." Benny wept like an orphaned child. Suddenly the atmosphere shifted, he had touched the hearts of the entire congregation. Some tried to keep from displaying emotion but couldn't. Most began to weep openly. "I love you," Benny continued as he looked out over the congregation. "I love you all very much. It's true that I can't get a job like other boys my age. I can't even go to a real school like all of you. At my school we just make baskets. But I can love you." Wiping tears, Benny added, "And I can pray for you. Just remember; if you get discouraged, Benny is praying for you. Anybody can pray."[6]

REVIEW It

1. What are the two most important prayer-life starters mentioned in this chapter?
2. Review the ten activities of prayer suggested as activities in a prayer room.
3. What are the eight suggestions for the creation of a prayer list? Add others you might think of.
4. Review the idea of "_____" and "happiness" as partners.
5. Review the sectors of the city – and determine who in your study group, among your family and friends, possibly even your church or fellowship, works with or in, or connects in some way with those sectors. That is the mission field with which you engage. It is where your missionary friends are located. It is the harvest field in which they labor. They will spend a few hours each week in worship with other believers, but they will spend multiplied hours at their jobs with believers from other congregations and non-believers.

TALK About It

1. Discuss the idea of creating a prayer room or space. Share with each other how you have accomplished that goal.
2. Of the ten activities suggested for personal prayer, which stands out to you as most important? Which have you never tried? Are there any you don't understand?
3. From the suggestions in this chapter, develop a prayer list. You may want to make this the beginning of a journal.
4. Discuss the "12 Additional Tips." Which do you think are most important? Pick three.

5. From the first two chapters of this book, what have you learned that has been most helpful?

Endnotes

1. Cleland B. McAfee, *There Is A Place of Quiet Rest* (Public Domain, 1903). He wrote these words after two of his nieces died from diphtheria. The Park College choir sang the new hymn outside the quarantined house. library.timelesstruths.org/music/Near_to_the_Heart_of_God/
2. E. M. Bounds, *Power Through Prayer* (Chicago: Moody, 2009), 54.
3. Ibid.
4. Adapted from a post by Glenn Wilson: "8 Important Things to Pray For." burtpresbyteran.blogspot.com/2010/07/eight-important-things-for-you-to-pray.html.
5. Adapted from Greg Qualls, "Spiritual Disciplines – Six Tips for Talking to God." gregqualls.com/tag/bible/.
6. Dick Eastman, *The Purple Pig* (Lake Mary, FL: Charisma House, Strang Communications; 2010), 37-38.

REVIEW It Answers

1. A PLACE and a TIME
2. Read Scripture; Rehearse God's Goodness; Commune with God; Present Your Needs; Praise; Intercede for Others; Pray Specifically; Pray Aloud; Listen; Pray Early
3. Character; Actions – That You Do No Evil; Love; The Unsaved; Grace Toward Others; Open Doors; Peace of Jerusalem; Leaders
4. Holiness

Angels your march oppose,
Who still in strength excel,
Your secret, sworn, eternal foes,
Countless, invisible.
With rage that never ends
Their hellish arts they try;
Legions of dire malicious fiends,
And spirits enthroned on high.

On earth the usurpers reign,
Exert their baneful power,
O'er the poor fallen sons of men
They tyrannize their hour:
But shall believers fear?
But shall believers fly?
Or see the bloody cross appear,
And all their power defy?

Jesus' tremendous Name
Puts all our foes to flight:
Jesus, the meek, the angry Lamb,
A Lion is in fight.
By all hell's host withstood,
We all hell's host o'erthrow;
And conquering them, through Jesus' blood,
We still to conquer go.

Our Captain leads us on;
He beckons from the skies,
And reaches out a starry crown,
And bids us take the prize:
"Be faithful unto death;
Partake My victory;
And thou shalt wear this glorious wreath.
And thou shalt reign with Me."[1]

CHAPTER THREE
The Privilege of Petitioning Heaven

Perspective: Prayer is bigger than merely asking! Though it certainly includes the privilege of offering prayer requests, God, due to His own nature, His investment in us as Creator and Redeemer, invites us to share our needs.

But the heart of prayer is the very relationship itself that permits and encourages us to ask God to do things for us, not as a distant deity, but as our Father. Imagine – we can ask God to do things for us. What a deal! What a privilege!

And yet, the heart of prayer, its highest calling, is not found in petitioning heaven, but in our gentle and daily communion with the benevolent God, made possible through the finished work of Christ on the cross and the indwelling Holy Spirit. Because of that new relationship, we are allowed to make requests for ourselves (petition) and others (intercession), in the name of Jesus.

This great privilege is afforded only by Christian prayer. Such a glorious benefit should always be partnered with gratitude.

"What Jesus did on the cross changed everything!"[2] From the moment the Holy Spirit flooded over and into the hearts of believers at Pentecost, in response to the acceptance and enthronement of Jesus in the heavens, his installation as our High Priest, we have direct access to God not experienced earlier by men, except Christ, since Adam. The Holy Spirit moved *inside* our souls – and became our prayer mentor, working from the inside out. This is why Jesus would say so emphatically, *"It is expedient for you that I go…"* (John 16:7)

The word *expedient* is translated, "to your advantage," profitable for you. The compound word, *symphérō,* means to bring or carry and do so "together with." To conjoin components so that they interact together to produce a profit, to advance a cause, to gain some advantage or result in a positive benefit. Jesus brought together sinful, imperfect man and a holy God, lost souls and the Father. In the new arrangement, we pray with the aid of the Spirit, and do so along with Jesus – *symphérō.* From this word, we derive symphony, which means to "sound together." Every prayer and every petition do not have to sound the same. Prayer, like a symphony, needs variety. And yet, a diversity of sound bound together by the same rhythm and supporting the same melody – Christ himself. A whole new dynamic has come to prayer, its privileges have been expanded and its scope enlarged. Its reach extended and its ease immeasurably improved. There are new rules about talking to God and hearing from God, pleasant rules. Prayer is now "an inside job."[3] Direct access to God is the option of every believer. It is only through believing prayer and by no other means that the kingdom of God advances. All our activities, to be effective, must be paired with prayer.

Double Trouble City

Charles Kuralt was a Carolina boy known for his "On the Road" television specials that always had a homey flavor. He found exotic, out-of-the-way people and places – like *Hell-for-Certain,* Kentucky; *Gnaw Bone,* Indiana; and *Why-Not,* North Carolina.[4] Of course, there are dozens of cities and towns with exotic names. If you want excitement, you can visit *Cyclone,* Texas; *Storms,* Ohio or *Hurricane,* Utah. You can join the celebration down in *Hoop and Holler,* Texas or settle into a milder place like *Boring or Barren,* found respectively in Oregon and Kentucky. There's *Trouble Street* in New York City, across the bay *Double Trouble,* in New Jersey. Wherever you live, troubles will find you.

Pain Triggers for Prayer

In Psalms 107, there are four things that trigger prayer requests:

1. **Emergencies** (interruptions to the rhythm and flow of daily life). *"Hungry and thirsty, their soul fainted in them. Then they cried out to the LORD in their trouble. And He delivered them out of their distresses. And He led them forth by the right way..."* (107:5-7 KJV). Here is the felt need, the spiritual weakness, the prayer and the answer.

2. **Bondage** (forces that threaten our freedom), death (loss of life and permanent separations). People...

    > *...sat in darkness and in the shadow of death, bound in affliction and irons – because they rebelled against the words of God, and despised the counsel of the Most High, Therefore He brought down their heart with labor; they fell down, and there was none to help. Then they cried out to the LORD in their trouble, and He saved them out of their distresses. He brought them out of darkness and the shadow of death, And broke their chains in pieces* (107:10-14 KJV).

    Here is the sad end of spiritual rebellion – darkness, bondage, abandonment – and then a turning back to God with salvation and liberation.

3. **Illness** (possibly death, largely self-inflicted, and yet still met with mercy). In captivity, the people grew ill. They were spiritually sick, an affliction centered more in the soul than in the body. They lost all appetite for meat – *"their soul ab-*

horred all manner of meat." Without nourishment, they famished. *"They draw near unto the gates of death."* Then it finally occurred to them that their unfaithfulness was to blame and then God *"...sent His word, and healed them, and delivered them from their destructions".* They cried out to God, and He healed them (107: 17-22 KJV).

4. **Financial crises** (need, want, deprivation, lack of daily bread). *"Those who go down to the sea in ships, who do business on great waters"* are international business dealers. They shop the world. They are the suppliers to the wholesalers and retailers. With great profits come great risks. Suddenly, their uninsured ships with their most recent investments and profit potentials are in trouble. No one could have predicted such an event. The ships are caught in a relentless and destructive storm. *"They mount up to the heavens,"* the waves are like a tsunami. *"They go down again to the depths; their soul melts because of trouble."* Veteran sailors fear.

> *They reel to and fro, and stagger like a drunken man, and are at their wits' end. Then they cry out to the LORD in their trouble, and He brings them out of their distresses. He calms the storm, so that its waves are still. Then they are glad because they are quiet; so He guides them to their desired haven* (107:23-30 KJV).

Overwhelmed by nature's unpredictable force, they have only one place to turn – God. Humbled, desperate, they pray, and God hears them on the troubled waters, exerts his power over nature quieting wind and waves, and guides them to a haven. He answers the prayers of profiteering sailors – that is grace.

Someone has said, "The most frightening sound in the world is a telephone ringing in the middle of the night."[5] When trouble comes, God does not want us to struggle alone. He urges us to invite Him into our battles. *"Let your requests be made known!"* Paul exhorts. Here is the invitation to share our needs with God. Sadly, we have developed a pattern of first sharing our needs with others. The first place we must go when we are in trouble is to God.

A Blessed Nation

In the USA, we have it so good that when the smallest thing goes bad, we catastrophize. We have conquered raging rivers with our elaborate dam systems, and wiped out life threatening childhood diseases. We moved from the horse and buggy as the principle means of transportation to manned missions to the moon and back. From simple frame houses with 'a path' to homes our grandparents could have hardly dreamed of with carpet-covered floors, central heat and air, microwave ovens, and remotely controlled digital televisions that we regulate from a vibrating recliner – all in the space of virtually one lifetime. My grandchildren find it difficult to believe that when I was a child, most television programs were only in black-and-white with no programming after midnight. During daytime hours, only a few channels were available and a good signal often required a major struggle with "rabbit ears". To change a channel, one had to walk all the way across the room. How primitive.

We have created paradise. We are so prosperous and dominant that the wars of the last six decades have required little sacrifice at home. Even as sons and daughters die abroad, we continue as if we were in peace-time as a nation. Those who lived through previous wars could never have imagined such a thing. We have developed the narcissistic conviction that nothing should affect our lives, diminish our personal liberty, limit our wants or will. The majority of the world knows no such enclave from life's hazards and menaces. And here in America, that is beginning to change.

A Battered World

"The new millennium began with much of the world consumed

in armed conflict or cultivating an uncertain peace."[6] In 2005, there were eight major wars under way, apart from some two dozen minor skirmishes. Two years earlier that figure had been 50 percent higher. Each year, tensions rise in the Middle East, and it seems that the whole region may erupt in conflict. We move from one terrorist threat to another, different, more sophisticated, and more lethal. Those who live on our southern border suggest a near war with the drug cartel is already in progress. Yet, in most of America, life goes happily, blindly on.

Consider this: If the whole world were a village of 100, 80 would live in substandard housing, and a significant number of those would live on the streets. Fifty would suffer from malnutrition, 33 would not have access to clean, safe drinking water. Twenty-four would not have any electricity. Of those with electricity, the vast majority would use it only for light at night. An estimated 90% of the world's population would find life in the typical American garage better living space than their present home. If you have food in the refrigerator, clothes on your back, a roof overhead, a place to sleep tonight, you are among the top 75 percent of people on the planet in terms of comfort. If you have money in the bank, in your wallet, and spare change in your pocket, you are among the top 8 percent of the wealthy in the world. Yet, we are plagued with worry.

In comparison with most of the world, we live in Utopia. Persecution of Christians in many nations of the world is unthinkable. According to the World Christian Encyclopedia, from A.D. 33 to 1914, 24 million Christians died for their faith – an unheralded fact. Even more shocking is that since A.D. 1915, in the last 100 years, an additional 45 million Christians have died for their faith around the world. This means that more Christians were martyred in the last century than all the previous centuries combined. Today over 400 Christians will die for their faith in Christ somewhere on the planet – 16 every hour, one every 3.5 minutes. Some 500 million people, one in 14, have experienced imprisonment, torture, starvation or war. Three billion live in areas where attendance at a church may endanger their lives.

Augustine declared, "People travel to wonder at the height of mountains, at the huge waves of the sea, at the long courses of the rivers, at the vast compass of the ocean, at the circular motion of the stars – and they pass by themselves without wondering."[7] The great crowning moment in creation was not Victoria Falls or the Grand Canyon, not the Swiss Alps or the winding Amazon. It was the moment God imprinted His image on the creature man, male and female. Then, joining them, he created family that also bears His image, and *He blessed them* (Gen. 1:28). Made only a bit lower than the angels, humanity was the zenith of God's work. You and I have not wondered until we have humbly wondered over the connection between ourselves and God. The earth is not our mother. God is our Father.

Bennan Manning suggests that, by and large, our generation has lost its sense of wonder. We are too grown up. We no longer catch our breath at the sight of a rainbow or the scent of a rose. Our inflated self makes us seem bigger and everything else is smaller, less impressive. We are blasé, worldly wise and sophisticated. We no longer run our fingers through water, shout at the stars or make faces at the moon. Water is H_2O, the stars have been classified and the moon is not made of green cheese. Thanks to satellite TV and the shrinking planet, we can visit places available in the past only to daring explorers. Manning says, "There was a time in the not too distant past when a thunderstorm caused men to shudder and feel small".[8] Science has stripped wonder of its awe. Meteorology reduces tornadoes to the dynamics created by cold and warm moist air caught up in the swirling jet stream; and then to an alpha-numeric scale. An 'F-5' that leaves a trail of destruction is reduced to a letter and a number, all easily explainable. We assure ourselves that one day better predictions and warning systems, along with stricter building codes and stronger structures will allow us to withstand the most intense of storms. We imagine ourselves as ultimately invincible. Such triumph, were it achievable, may be the ultimate loss. Abraham Heschel reminds us, "As civilization advances, the sense of wonder declines…"[9]

Once we rolled up our sleeves and growled back at nature, picking up the debris of hurricanes and tornadoes, providing relief for the world, rebuilding in a matter of months, planting and renewing, smiling and swelling with pride that we were innovative and resourceful, wise and able to match nature's wrath with equal resolve. We are delusional.[10] A few years ago, an earthquake and tsunami devastated Japan. In this nation, a vicious outbreak of tornadoes affected six southern states. A Northeastern hurricane crippled New York and New Jersey with monstrous devastation. New Orleans, years after Katrina, left whole streets with empty houses. Haiti has not fully recovered from its deadly earthquake. A recent Mississippi flood was the worst in 80 years with small rural farm communities intentionally flooded to save larger cities in an area of devastation that stretched from Memphis to New Orleans. The earth reels. Nature is vicious. Sin and death have infected the cosmos itself. It will not be tamed until Christ, the Creator and Redeemer returns. We need God.

Blinding Sight

In 1820, a young child, six weeks old caught a cold in her eyes. A doctor unwisely prescribed a mustard poultice, and Fanny Crosby would be virtually blind the rest of her life. The dark world in which she was trapped only made her more resilient, "O what a happy soul I am! Although I cannot see, I am resolved that in this world contented I will be." That declaration came at the age of eight. She would spend a great deal of time in New York's Institution for the Blind as a student, then as a teacher, and finally as a writer-in-residence. At first, her preoccupation was poetry. She gained the attention of both Congress and of Presidents, the rich and famous came to see her. At the age of 31, she attended a revival meeting and met Jesus Christ. As the congregation sang, *"Alas and did my Savior bleed?"* she was deeply moved. When the line came, *"Here Lord, I give myself away,"* she recalled how her heart was flooded with heavenly joy. It would be 14 more years before a hymnist partnered with her to begin to put her poetic words to music. Over the next five decades, she wrote 8,000 hymns.[11] "Blindness," she wrote in later life, "cannot keep the sunlight of hope from the trustful soul."[12] She would say if she had a choice now, in retrospect, she would want to be born blind.

What do we really have to complain about? Sadly, in light of the larger needs of our brothers and sisters around the world, the things about which we pray are often slight. And yet, God invites us to pray about everything. He never says, "Your needs are not worth considering!" James, the brother of Jesus said, *"He upbraids not!"* (James 1:15). He does not reproach or censure. He does not rebuke or treat us harshly for coming with needs. He welcomes us!

Any Prayer Requests?

In my growing up years, I remember the words – "Any prayer requests?" A litany of needs would pour forth. Unspoken requests were made known "by the lifting of a hand." It happened in virtually every service – prayer request time. Yet in all those years, I never recall a message or instruction on 'prayer requests'. Never do I recall hearing a teaching on the larger context of this passage. How do we present prayer needs to the Lord? Are there principles to be partnered with our petitions? Is something required of us other than prayer? The Bible assures us that God hears, and we know that prayer and praise combined elicit his intervention.[13] But in Philippians 4:4-9, there are principles connected with the presentation of prayer requests, a kind of formula, and more importantly, an eye-opening outcome beyond mere answers that God anticipates from us.

Faith in the Midst of Fiery Trouble

Scripture is consumed with the idea of God *receiving praise* and *glory*. In contrast, we are too often consumed with the idea of God *relieving our pain* and solving our problems. *We* pray in order to be released *from* trouble. God wants us to triumph *in the midst* of trouble. *"In the world,"* Jesus promised, *"You will have tribulation"* (John 16:33). It's a promise. We are not exempted from life's problems. *"The rain falls on the just and the unjust"* (Matthew 5:45). Yet, simultaneous with tribulation, Jesus promised *"…in Me, you will have peace"* (John 16:33). There is a place of peace, a relationship with the resurrected Christ by the indwelling presence of the Spirit where we can live in peace, even while the storm is raging around us. Jesus is the eye in the middle of life's destructive storms.

Herb Caen, a *San Francisco Chronicle* columnist, wrote, "Every morning in Africa, a gazelle wakes up knowing it must run faster than the fastest lion or die. Every morning a lion wakes up knowing it must outrun the slowest gazelle or starve. It doesn't matter whether you are a lion or a gazelle, when the sun comes up, you'd better be running!"[14] The cheetah can sprint up to 70 miles per hour, but it cannot sustain the speed. It must overtake its prey in the first burst of speed because its heart is too small to allow an extended chase. An undersized heart is a problem, not only for cheetahs, but also for Christians.[15] Roman authorities would learn that when Christians sang to the lions, the effect on the worldly crowd was chilling! Paul cites four factors of a quality witness before a watching world.

Four Factors in a Quality Witness

1. **Joy** – *"Rejoice in the Lord, always!"* This requires a decision to live joyfully, regardless of outer circumstances. And to be verbal, to give voice to joy. We are not to be a silent witness.

2. **Moderation** – *"Let your moderation (gentleness, poise) be made known to all men"* (KJV). A gracious gentleness. This disposition is to be extended to all men at all times. This seems a humanly impossible ideal.

3. **Attitude of gratitude** – *"In everything, by prayer and supplication, with thanksgiving..."* We are to be thankful, actively offering acknowledgements to God for provision and watchful care. "Thanks" to God are given even in the face of problems. Gratitude is to be openly expressed before men. Thanksgiving is our way of bragging on God! It is a powerful means of evangelism.

4. **Peace** – *"And the peace of God which surpasses understanding shall guard your heart and minds."* Peace is the environment in which we live. Notice the four – joy, gentleness, gratitude and peace. An underpinning of peace. A practice of gratitude. A posture of graciousness. A disposition of joy. Of those, joy and gratitude, are noisy! Gentleness and peace are quiet. All four evidence the life of Christ in us and our confidence in his delivering power.

REVIEW It

1. The heart of prayer is not petition, but _____.
2. The term for "making requests" of God is _____.
3. Praying or petitioning for others is called _____.
4. All prayer is to be wrapped in _____.
5. What are the four triggers for prayer needs according to Psalms 187? _____, bondage, _____, _____ crisis.

TALK About It

1. We pray to be relieved from trouble; God wants us to triumph in the midst of trouble. True or false? Agree or disagree?

2. Discuss the Four Factors of a Quality Witness.

3. Talk about our silence – or little joy or gratitude in the midst of the trial or after a breakthrough. What impact does that have on our witness?

4. Have you seen prayer primarily or narrowly as 'asking of God,' and missed the bigger prayer picture? That prayer is at its heart 'communion' with God? And the 'great exchange' is connected with our witness before men?

5. How is your prayer life doing?

Endnotes

1. Charles Wesley, "Angels Your March Oppose!" (Hymns and Sacred Poems, 1749). See also: www.hymnlyrics.org/newlyrics_a/angelsyourmarchoppose.php. Copyright by Creative Commons: creativecommons.org/licenses/by-sa/3.0/

2. David Bordon, *Discover the Power in the Prayers of Paul* (Tulsa, OK: Harrison House, 2005), xi.

3. Ibid, xvi.

4. Charles Kuralt, "On the Road with Charles Kuralt," *American Names* (New York: Fawcett Gold Metal; 1985), 192-195.

5. Ibid, 71.

6. Natsu Taylor Saito, *Meeting the Enemy: American Exceptionalism and International Law* (New York: NYU Press, 2010), 222.

7. David Foster, *Accept No Mediocre Life: Living Beyond Labels, Libels, and Limitations* (Faithwords, 2007), 17.

8. Brennan Manning, *The Importance of Being Foolish: How to Think Like Jesus* (Zondervan, 2006), 16.

9. Abraham Heschel, *God in Search of Man: A Philosophy of Judaism* (Macmillan, 1976), 46.

10. Elizabeth Kea, Editor, *Amazed by Grace;* Section: "The Grace of Wonder" by Brennan Mannning (Nashville, TN: Thomas Nelson Publishing, The W Publishing Group; 2003), 157-158.

11. Robert Morgan, *On This Day* (Nashville, TN: Thomas Nelson Publishers, 1997), 2-15.
12. www.wholesomewords.org/biography/bcrosby8.html.
13. Ben A. Jennings, *The Arena of Prayer: Learn the Secrets of the World's Greatest Privilege – Prayer* (Orlando, FL: New Life Publications, 1999), 73; Barnes notes on James 1:15, found at www.biblos.com.
14. Foster, 198.
15. Ibid.

REVIEW It Answers

1. Communion
2. Petition
3. Intercession
4. Thanksgiving
5. Emergencies, Bondage, Illness/Death, Financial Crises

I once was lost in sin, but Jesus took me in,
And then a little light from heaven filled my soul;
It bathed my heart in love and wrote my name above,
And just a little talk with Jesus makes me whole.

Now let us, Have a little talk with Jesus,
Let us, tell Him all about our troubles,
He will hear our faintest cry,
And He will, answer by and by;
Now when you,
Feel a little pray'r wheel turning,
And you, know a little fire is burning.
You will, Find a little talk with Jesus makes it right.

Sometimes my path seems drear,
without a ray of cheer,
And then a cloud of doubt
may hide the light of day;
The mists of sin may rise and hide the starry skies,
But Just a little talk with Jesus clears the way.

I may have doubts and fears,
my eyes be filled with tears,
But Jesus is a friend who watches day and night;
I go to him in prayer, He knows my every care,
And Just a little talk with Jesus makes it right.[1]

CHAPTER FOUR
Meet the Christians: They Live on Peace Street

And the peace of God, which surpasses all understanding,
will guard your hearts and minds through Christ Jesus.

Perspective: It is the God of peace who gives the gift of peace. And it is in this peace that we stand, and out of this peace that we witness and minister. "My peace I give to you." Jesus lived in a bubble of peace – and so should we. A demeanor of peace is an extraordinary witness. Our sinful debt has been graciously settled with a holy God. We are not under condemnation. We have been given immunity. We are in an incredibly powerful place to be a witness. As trouble comes, and peace guards and keeps us, people watch in amazement. Grace sustains us. We are living "the great exchange" – peace in the midst of the world's problems.

Case Study

Joe and Julie Christian are wonderful believers. Joe has some job issues. His plant is downsizing and may close. His father recently died. Julie has been chronically sick. Her sister went through a divorce and is now living with them. At the same time, their church is in a season of transition. None of these things are necessarily the direct doings of Satan or one of his minions. Yet, in such a context of change and uncertainty, turmoil and trouble, the devil does his finest work.

This is what we might call a "warfare zone." Joe and Julie are in the nexus of a series of life calamities. Satan, like an ambulance chasing attorney, shows up in the middle of such stressful scenes, passing out his calling card and offering his diabolical counsel. Under such pressure, Joe and Julie need God's direct protection and care. The enemy would like to use this moment to extinguish their light! He desires that they stumble, fall, or lose faith altogether. That they give up! Split up! That they doubt God and have a faith-collapse in front of family and friends.

The Lord wants precisely the opposite. He wants their light to shine, especially in this crisis moment. He wants to reveal through them that He is an alive, prayer-answering God. He wants them to find grace to stand in peace, strong in their faith. He wants this experience to deepen their determination, causing them to pull together, to believe in the face of difficulty and stand as a staunch witness to watching friends.

The Promises Applied: Susana Wesley would say, "God's promises are sealed to us, but not dated."[2] Jesus promised that in spite of the "tribulation" the world would bring, that we would find "peace" in the middle of the trouble (John 16:33). God wants Joe and Julie to discover a bubble of peace in the middle of their storm. Witness is not something we *do,* before it is first something that we *are!* Neither Joe and Julie, nor you and I, can effectively do witnessing unless we effectively live as a witness. When the Holy Spirit comes, His purpose is to give us the power to be witnesses! Our lives then are to offer evidentiary proof of the resurrection (overcoming power), the enthronement (acceptance in heaven) of Jesus.

The Power Appropriated: Jesus overcame death, and He gives us the power to triumph over death's morphed forms, things that claim our life, joy and peace, threaten unity and instill fear. *"We are more than conquerors!"* (Romans 8:37). With Paul we declare, *"None of these things move us!"* (Acts 20:24). We evidence, here and now, the power of the resurrection. We also celebrate, by the enthronement of Christ in the heavens, a new level of acceptance in God. We have a stronger bond and higher standing. We are the bride-partner of the Lord of lords and the King of kings. We are children of the Most High God, adopted into his family. We live out of this triumph, secure in His acceptance.

This is more than theology. It is tangible at times, unquestionable and felt. On one side, our victory over the world and the devil is assured; on the other, our renewed relationship with the Father, through the Son, is sealed. On one hand, the past has been dealt with – we are free of sin's chains and its penalty, from the grip and the guilt, and therefore, death's hold; on the other hand, our future is inestimable, unfathomable. We will rule and reign with Christ on the earth. We will see the desert blossom like a rose. We will experience a thousand annual celebrations of the Feast of Tabernacles in Jerusalem.

The Prayer That Sustains: Prayer sustains our witness as we live in unbroken fellowship with God. All the trials and tribulations, whether they come randomly by living in this fallen world or they get a push from the Evil One, have the potential of separating us from the love of God if allowed. Ephesians 6 is not only a spiritual warfare passage; it is fundamentally a prayer passage! The only way we survive the warfare waged against us is through prayer. God is for us, but victory is appropriated in prayer. There is a "having done all to stand" dimension to victory that requires an investment on our part. "Having done all," we are assured, we can and will stay on our feet, overcoming (Ephesians 6:13). If we do not 'pray through' the crisis, with passion and by the enabling of the Spirit, we have not 'done all' and we may not stand. "Prayer is measured, not by time, but by intensity."[3]

> *If God is for us, who can be against us?... Who shall separate us from the love of Christ? Shall tribulation, or distress, or persecution, or famine, or nakedness, or peril, or sword?...In all these things we are more than conquerors through Him who loved us...Neither death nor life, angels or principalities or powers, things present or things to come, not height or depth, or any other created thing shall be able to separate us from the love of God* (Romans 8:31-37).

People who have a sense of *mastery* over life, who have learned to resist a victim mentality and retain an overcoming perspective, a feeling of being in control despite the circumstances, have a 60 percent lower risk of death when compared to those who feel hopeless and helpless in the face of some life challenge.[4]

The Place of Rest: Prayer should be passionate. And prayer should be the essence of peace and rest. God created the earth and all in it in six days – and then He rested. The crowning end of creation was rest. The last creature created on the sixth day was man, so the first full day for Adam and Eve was a day of rest. They were charged with cultivating and guarding the garden, but their first order of business was rest! In fact, even on the sixth day, Adam is induced to sleep – an afternoon nap. And during that time of rest, God acted in his behalf, creating arguably Adam's greatest gift – Eve.

Rest is a form of prayer. In the creation narrative, the model offered us is that one entire day a week was to be given to prayerful rest, to time with God for inner renewal. The *Sabbath* was not to be supra-spiritual. Normal life is to be lived with an awareness of God's presence. We were created with this need for physical and spiritual rest. The law reversed the process, *"Six days shall you labor and on the seventh, shall you rest."* (Exodus 20:9) In the Creation order, we were invited into God's rest – rest with a forward view. It was preparation for the coming week. Man now was to be the creative one, replicating God's behavior – growing and guarding the garden. Under the law, with the fall of man, the process was reversed. Man now had to earn his right to rest after six days of labor. Rest was recovered, but with a backward view. He entered the Sabbath, as a seventh day, not as a first full day out of rest.

When Jesus came, He reversed the order. He labored and then called us into rest, *"My yoke is easy, my burden is light"* (Matthew 11:30). We worship, not on the Sabbath, but on the day of resurrection, the first day of the week. That is our Sabbath – and yet, Sabbath is no longer merely a day! It is a way of life. In the new order, out of grace, we begin our week with God, entering into His rest, and then laboring out of rest. This is God's way – begin with prayerful rest.

In our fast-paced world, we live off caffeine and adrenaline. And adrenaline produces a high as powerful as morphine. It affects the body in much the same way, making use of the same receptors.[5] We are addicted to 'fast' – fast cars, fast 60-minute plots, fast money, fast sermons, fast prayers - fast! The thrill of a chase, the pursuit of the unknown, the new opportunity, the exotic experience, the unseen place. Rest is boring! A new goal quickly replaces another – so we pursue one carrot, then another. We are addicted to the chase. More precisely, to our inner stress hormones. They just lock onto a new target. Moving at 90 miles an hour, we have no idea that we are addicted to the chemicals in our own body.

STEP ONE: Let Peace Guard Your Heart and Mind

The peace of God, which surpasses all understanding, will guard your hearts and minds through Jesus Christ (Philippians 4:7)

1. Meet the Castle Guard – Peace. What an irony! Here is "peace" serving as a guard, a sentry, a soldier! Most people in the process of hiring a security guard to protect their home would not hire "Mr. Peace." Peace is too gentle and tame, too docile and non-violent for such a job. Who would hire a pacifist as a guard? Some would

49

hire a worldly, shoot-first-and-ask-questions-later type person. The castle guard that God offers us is peace! What a contradiction.

In order to take your house, any intruder must first dispose of your guard. Here is the logic: when peace is threatened, the clear indication is that you are under attack. When your peace is rattled, you are in some level of spiritual warfare or siege by the Evil One who has some malevolent purpose. When peace goes, so does joy. In such times,

Key Principle
Peace serves as our guard. When it is threatened, it is the clearest first indicator of your being in a warfare zone.

we may lose our emotional equilibrium and poise, and act in less than gentle and gracious ways. We are absorbed by the problem. Our witness is diminished.

2. Meet the Aggressor – Worry. The subtext of the passage is that of trouble. When worry assaults our minds and hearts, not only is our peace disturbed, our sense of God's nearness is also affected. The sound of our joy is silenced. We may panic, become short-tempered, sensitive and reactionary. We disqualify our witness. We may feel that God is no longer guarding us. How do we prevent this loss of joy and grace? How do we stop the violation of protective peace? We can't exempt ourselves from problems. After all, life happens! But there is a place beyond the reach of the Evil One.

Joy, grace and peace are companions God offers the believer. Of these, peace is the more militant, much more so than joy or grace. It serves as the sentry, like an armed soldier guarding our hearts and minds. A troubled mind is an indication that 'peace' is under attack. Some problem has effectively penetrated our defenses. Some worry is about to take our hearts captive. The loss of peace threatens joy and grace. When peace goes, quickly bar the doors of your heart. Cry out to God. Be vigilant.

3. Meet the Militant Protector – the Peace of God. It is a paradox that "peace" should be the guard, the militant one. But the Bible says, peace "shall mount guard."[6] What irony. The peace of God protects, like an armed watchman, vigilant and aware. The word *guard* carries the idea of a posted soldier.[7] Inner peace is a gift from God. *"My peace, I give to you"* (John 14:27). However, once given, you must conscientiously monitor your peace level. This peace came at the moment of conversion. The guilt of sin rolled away. The cares of the world were severed. Our enmity with God ended. Reconciliation took place. We were no longer at war with God, others or ourselves, due to sin.

Through the Christ of the cross, we have peace *with* God. And peace with God invites the peace *of* God. And the power behind that peace is "the God of peace" Himself. *"The God of peace will be with you."* Wow! *"The Lord,"* we were told in verse five *"will be with you."* And where He is – peace and safety can be found. Moses exhorted the people, *"Don't be afraid! Stand still, and see what the LORD will do to save you today"* (Exodus 14:13, GWT).

4. Meet the Gateway to Security – the Rest of God. The Eastern Church and their more modern writer-counterparts, such as Henri Nouwen, emphasize the importance of "coming to rest" in prayer. Nouwen says, *"Hesychia,* the rest which flows from unceasing prayer, needs to be sought at all costs, even when the flesh is itchy, the world alluring, and the demons noisy."[8] Perseverance is the price necessary to return to a state of peace, even if that place is the eye of the storm itself. Peace, inner rest, is the goal. This is not external peace. It is not mere coexistence with a problem. This is not avoidance, but violent faith in the face of any impending danger or challenge to our confidence in God. It is the ability to live in the storm, without letting the storm inside of you.

A Panoramic View

Look at the landscape of the entire passage. It begins with a call to *"Rejoice in the Lord, always!"* No matter what the problem or how great the pain, we present our needs and requests to God, and in doing so we preserve our "moderation" and poise, or as the King James says, our "gentleness or graciousness." Joy, poise and peace. What a picture. On one side of pulsating needs is joy. On the other side is peace, with moderation or steadiness in the middle. Here is the wonderful Christian trio – joy, grace and peace.

This peace is beyond all comprehension, all under-standing, literally beyond "all mind!" It is beyond our "thinking power."[9] *"The Lord will keep him in perfect peace whose mind is stayed on Thee"* (Isaiah 26:3, KJV). "Keep" means to defend. The idea is of a fort, a garrison or a wall of protection. This peace "will keep you in Christ." It will "…prevent you from going out of Christ."[10] When we are threatened by spiritual warfare, peace is the enclave, a safe house.

With our minds overloaded and fixated on problems, fear pushes faith to the background. Harmony is drowned out by dissonant sounds – the banging drums and the clanging symbols of the world. "In such moments, our only solution is to clear the stage of our mind, tune out the things of the world and hear heaven's music. Christ Himself should come to the center stage of our mind."[11] We are reminded, *"As a man thinks in his heart, so is he…"* (Proverbs 23:7). The term heart indicates the thoughts and the action prompts of the mind![12]

Though the world promises tribulation, the God of peace promises that such troubles are not eternal. He will bruise Satan under our feet (Romans 16:20) – surely, certainly, and shortly. In the meantime, we are to fight with the weapon of peace, with our feet shod with the preparation of the gospel of peace (Ephesians 6:15). It is the only way we can stay on our feet. In a battle, if you cannot stay on your feet, you may not only suffer defeated, but you may be slain. To stay on your feet, stand in peace. Lose peace, and you lose the battle.

Barbara and I raised five children – all different. Cheryl, our second, had an irritating habit. It worried me a bit when she was young. When a frightening storm arose or she faced an overwhelming problem, she would announce, "I am going to sleep." And she did. I feared some developing phobia, a pattern of escape from reality. I wanted to her sit up with the rest of us, and bite her nails with us, as the thunder rattled the windows and the lightning danced around us. Now that she is grown, and I am only slightly wiser, I wish I could grow up to be like her. Be responsible. Do your best. Then sleep in peace. God is awake.

Review It

1. Behind the peace of God is the God of _____.
2. As peace goes, so goes the _____.
3. The Holy Spirit came in connection to persistent prayer (Acts 1-2), and His purpose was to make of us a _____ (Acts 1:8).
4. The nexus of spiritual warfare is in our _____.
5. Roman soldiers had special footwear for battle, shoes fitted with cleats that allowed them to retain their footing in warfare. Our feet are to be fitted with the readiness, the preparation, of the _____.

Talk About It

1. What does the peace of God – contentment – mean?
2. Discuss the idea of peace as a guard – and its "capture" as a first indicator of warfare.
3. How can we understand spiritual warfare as a mental process?

4. Review the idea of 'the heart' as more than an organ. Ever had your heart stop? Skip a beat at the mention of some surprising news?

5. When you are in a tailspin – can you let go? Trust your faith? Will God really fly the plane?

6. Examine Ephesians 6 as a "prayer" passage.

Endnotes

1. Cleavant Derrick, *Just a Little Talk with Jesus* (Music Corporation of America, Publisher; Stamps Baxter Publishing, 1937).
2. Quote by Susana Wesley. John Whitehead, Thomas Hewlings Stockton, *The Life of the Rev. John Wesley* (Stephen Couchman: London; 1892), 44.
3. *The Kneeling Christian*, 73.
4. B. W. Penninx, T. Van Tilburg, D. M. Kriegsman, etc., "Effects of Social Support and Personal Coping Resources on Mortality in Older Age: The Longitudinal Aging Study Amsterdam," (American Journal of Epidemiology, 146; 1997), 510-519.
5. Don Colbert, *Deadly Emotions: Understand the Mind-Body-Spirit Connection That Can Heal Or Destroy You* (Nashville, TN: Thomas Nelson, 2006), 31.
6. Kenneth Samuel Wuest, *Word Studies in the Greek New Testament* (Grand Rapids, MI: William B. Eerdmans, 1953), 110.
7. M. R. Vincent, *Vincent's Word Studies on the New Testament* (Peabody, MA: Hendrickson Publishers, 1985), 891.
8. Quoted by Peter Greig and David Roberts, *Red Moon Rising – How 24-7 Prayer is Awakening a Generation* (Eastbourne, England: Relevant Books, Kingsway Publications; 2003), 68.
9. H. C. G. Moule. *Studies in Philippians* (Grand Rapids, MI: Kregel; 1977), 113.
10. Ibid.
11. Charles L. Allen, *All Things Are Possible Through Prayer: The Faith-Filled Guidebook That Can Change Your Life* (Baker Publishing Group, 1978), 44.
12. H. C. G. Moule. *Studies in Philippians* (Grand Rapids, MI: Kregel; 1977), 114.

Review It Answers

1. Peace
2. Battle
3. Witness
4. Mind
5. Gospel or Good News of Peace. Some suggest the Gospel of Reconciliation.

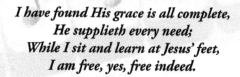

I have found His grace is all complete,
He supplieth every need;
While I sit and learn at Jesus' feet,
I am free, yes, free indeed.

It is joy unspeakable and full of glory,
Full of glory, full of glory;
It is joy unspeakable and full of glory,
Oh, the half has never yet been told.
I have found the pleasure I once craved,
It is joy and peace within;
What a wondrous blessing, I am saved
From the awful gulf of sin.
I have found that hope so bright and clear,
Living in the realm of grace;
Oh, the Savior's presence is so near,
I can see His smiling face.
I have found the joy no tongue can tell,
How its waves of glory roll;
It is like a great o'er flowing well,
Springing up within my soul.[1]

CHAPTER FIVE
Step Two: Take the Disposition of Joy

Rejoice in the Lord, always, again I say, rejoice!

Perspective: Why do we see holiness and happiness as opposites? Christianity and solemnity as partners? Joyous happy believers are far too rare! The Holy Days of the Old Testament were feast days, festivals. Yahweh loves a party. Jesus did too (Matthew 11:19; Luke 7:34). The absence of noisy Christian joy may be, in the midst of this troubled world, the greatest deficit in our witness to a watching world. This is not circumstantial joy, but that certain joy flowing out of the overcoming life of Jesus Himself, issuing from the throne of God. Joy! Without it, our witness is dull and lifeless. With it, our words are combined with music. With it, our smile and laughter are magnetic. With it, we evidence the certainty about which we testify.

Bruce recalled the Christmas season early in his marriage when he and his wife were a one-car family. She left early for the mountains of North Carolina with their small children. Work had demanded that he not leave until Christmas Eve. Arriving at the bus station, anxious to join his family, he found a long line waiting to board the bus. When it pulled into the station, the driver popped through the door and yelled, "Room for only three!" Bruce was not among the first three in line. He protested, "I purchased my ticket weeks ago." But holding a ticket didn't assure a seat. "First come, first served. No guarantees! Look at your ticket closely." Several people made it on. Then the driver yelled, "Room for one more!" Bruce was going to make it after all. He threw his suitcase into the baggage compartment. But once aboard, there was not a seat left. "Must have counted wrong young man, you'll have to get off."

His holiday spirit was gone. Flat. His jingle bells were busted. He crawled off the bus and headed into the bus station dejectedly dragging his bag. The ticket agent calculated the options. "Got a bus in here in 20 minutes. Gets you to D.C. From there you can catch a bus to…" It wasn't the destination Bruce wanted, but it was close enough. Twenty minutes later he boarded a nearly empty bus – what a contrast. He sunk down into his seat, still depressed. A quite senior lady lugged herself aboard and despite lots of room, she took the seat immediately across from Bruce. She was all alone – on Christmas Eve. She was obviously poor. For a moment, he was pulled from his self-obsession to consider the plight of this elderly soul. Then he descended back into self-ingratiating gloominess, but only momentarily.

As the bus pulled out, he could hear someone on the nearly vacant vehicle talking. Muttering. He glanced around. Everyone was sitting alone. Who could anyone be talking to? Then he realized it was the elderly woman directly across from him. She was engaged in a mumbling monologue – to herself. He pulled his hat over his head, sank down and determined to ignore her. But the sounds persisted. She then moved from soft murmurs to music. She was singing. Then she was talking again. No, he realized suddenly, she wasn't talking – she was praying.

"God, I thank you for providing this trip. I thank you for the occasion of the birth of your son Jesus. What a Savior!" And then she would begin to sing again. Praying and singing. Singing and praying –

miles of it! Bruce was convicted. Her circumstances, her poverty, her status in life could not drown out her noisy fruit – joy![2]

Ten Joy Principles

1. Joy – A Fire. "Joy," Helen Keller would say, "is the holy fire that keeps our purpose warm and our intelligence aglow." Paul urged, *"Rejoice in the Lord always. Again I say, rejoice!"* (Philippians 4:4). Remember, this is a prayer passage! Look at 'the context' of the passage. Every verse should be interpreted by the verses around it (context). Paul connects the idea of "prayer requests" to the larger image of our behavior before a watching world. He urges us to adopt the disposition of joy. We come into prayer loaded with pressing needs, and yet, Paul directs us to *"Rejoice in the Lord, always!"* It is a command, not even an option, if you are a serious disciple. He even repeats the command for emphasis, *"Again I say, 'Rejoice.'"*

Here is joy in the face of some urgent need, some pain or some plaguing problem. "The surest mark of a Christian is not faith, or even love, but joy," according to Samuel Shoemaker.[3] This joy is an expression of faith. It is evidence of our confidence that God will provide. Rather than being worried and anxious, we pray. This is a Biblical template for offering prayer requests to God that will garner an answer. And the process begins with joy.

2. Joy – A Fragrance. Richard Würmbrand wrote the book *Tortured for Christ*. No one seemed to believe the degree of horrors perpetrated by the Communists on Christians until he escaped from Romania and testified before a congressional hearing in Washington. He removed his shirt and revealed the ghastly scars from multiple beatings and persecution. His crime? He was a Christian pastor. His message, out of suffering, is convicting:

A flower, if you bruise it under your feet, rewards you by giving you its perfume. Likewise, Christians, tortured by the Communists, rewarded their torturers with love. We brought many of our jailors to Christ. And we are dominated by one desire: to give Communists who have made us suffer the best we have, the salvation which comes from our Lord Jesus Christ.[4]

It was *"for the joy that was set before him"* that Jesus endured the cross (Hebrews 12:1-2). *"Into your hands, I commend my Spirit."* Physically, he was on the cross and headed for the grave. But, spiritually, he was in the hands of the Father. You and I may face such measurable and palpable adversity that it seems tangible. The only relief is to see what is beyond it, that which God has set before us in another world, and to smell the fragrance of that place and here now, to put ourselves into the hands of God. Incense is the stuff of heaven; prayer is the means by which it produces love.

3. Joy – A Contrary, Subversive Force. Joy is subversive. When we might weep, instead, we sing. When others are fearful, we are steadied by faith. When others are despairing, we are confident and resolved. We don't know how. We don't know where. We don't know when – but we know God. Joy is the Spirit's noisy fruit, evidence of the Christ-life within us. We are noisy Christians who make 'happy sounds.'

There *is* such a thing as legitimate "holy laughter!" God's people are to be, as Demos Shakarian, the founder of Full Gospel Businessmen was fond of saying, "the happiest people on the face of the earth." When Sarah laughed at the announcement by the angel that she would have a child in the Spring, at the appointed time, the Angel of the Lord confronted her, *"Is there anything too hard for God?"* (Genesis 18:14). Abraham had believed, but Sarah had never allowed herself to believe that she would have a child. Sarah's laughter was doubtful optimism at best, or worse yet, cynicism shackled by unbelief.

People have dreams that could change their world, alter their lives, even redirect history, and their native response is cynical silent laughter. Messages of hope are met with silent sneers of disbelief. "It's okay for a preacher to believe that sort of thing. He lives in a different world than I do anyway." The cynical laughter assassinates the dream. It assails belief. It fractures faith. It immobilizes.

This time it would be different. Sarah's spontaneous burst of uncertain joy – "It can't be, could it be?" – was met with the angelic confrontation: "Did Sarah laugh?" It was enough to dislodge her from the place of utter unbelief. The long delayed child would be named Isaac – "laughter." Joy is often the means by which God nudges us out of silent cynicism. It is the means by which He breaks off the fetters of debilitating skepticism. Sarah's joy was an audible gasp, something reflexive from deep within that urged her to step over a line she had never dared to cross. It was a divinely planted longing, buried deep within her, one that was aligned with God's will, but had been repressed by uncertainty and doubt. She simply could not believe it was possible. Abraham dreamed; Sarah did not. He believed; she would never allow herself to do so. But deep inside, she too longed for the promised child. She longed to have the deadness in her live again. To dance with the impossible.[5]

Is God calling you to deeply laugh? To embrace the dream you thought was dead?

4. Joy – The Sound the Evil One Hates. The Evil One hates noisy, happy, genuine Christians! He does not want to see our gratitude expressed to God – either as an individual or a family, as a nation or community, that offers thanks to God for all He has done. Satan does not want to permit as much as one individual to say grace over a crust of bread. His goal is to silence us, to destroy our inner peace and have us be anything but steady and moderate, gentle and gracious under fire. Such a Christian – joyful and exuberant, steady under fire, always thankful, peaceful and calm, unruffled by the spiritual warfare around them – is an absolute terror to the kingdom of darkness. Luther, it is said, was awakened one night by a disturbance in his room. Wide awake and sitting up in his bed, Lucifer stood at his feet. Luther reportedly looked at the devil and muttered, "O, it's only you!" and went back to sleep.

When Leslie Town Hope came through Ellis Island in 1908, he was only four. A cruel skewing of his name, Les Hope, was rendered as "Hopeless." But the resilient lad would overcome the moniker. He would change his name and arguably become the greatest comedian, one of the most beloved characters of the twentieth century – Bob Hope.[6] He made jokes and provoked laughter at everyone and everything. The nation listened – and laughed. He was at his best when times seemed toughest. His jokes were a diversion from the deadly pressure of daily life. He told America that things could be worse – and everyone laughed, knowing he was right. But then Hope would suggest, things would soon be better – and everyone breathed a bit easier. He rallied performers and took them in war zones to offer 'Hope' to soldiers living with the threat of death itself. If there was a war, Bob Hope was going to get as close to the fire as possible – and laugh. We should too! Luther declared, "When I cannot pray, I always sing." Wesley, too, believed that, "Praise opens the door to more grace."[7] O, the power of joy.

5. Joy – The Sound the Hurting Need to Hear. No one maintained joy while dancing with death more than Mother Teresa, called the Saint of the Gutters. She organized the Missionaries of Charity. She oozed joy. Her birth place was Skopje, Macedonia. As a teen, she was led to Calcutta, India. There she spotted a dying woman lying in the street, alone, no longer able to fight off the rats. Barely alive, the noxious creatures had already started devouring her weak body. No one cared.

Stirred deeply, she remembers being compelled to act. Returning to the overcrowded city, the government gave her the use of a broken down building adjoining a Hindu temple. From that obscure place, she started a thankless ministry that would make her a household name around the world. That broken-down building became a place for the abandoned to die with care – the Home for the Dying. "If there is a God in heaven, and a Christ we love, nobody should die alone," she believed.[8] Living in a sea of diseased and dying people, she never lost her joy.

The West could not understand either her selflessness or her joy. All the things that spell happiness in our culture were absent – a typical home, a family, plenty, privacy and more. She lived on the edge of poverty, gave her time cleaning up the most vile and odorous humans imaginable, wiping body fluids from unconscious cancer and leprosy victims, all the while appearing blissful. Malcolm Muggeridge once interviewed her, asking her bluntly if her joy was a façade. "Is that a put-on?" Muggeridge asked. She replied, "Oh no, not at all. Nothing makes you happier than when you really reach out in mercy to someone who is badly hurt." Self-preoccupation is the route to despair. Happiness does not come from our acquisitions, but from our giving. Not the giving of mere things, but the giving of ourselves. Those who visited her facility would find the sisters joyfully singing.

6. Joy – The Sound of a Committed Christian. We rejoice… *"in the Lord!"* The phrase occurs earlier in the letter. *"In the Lord,"* we *"stand fast"* (4:1) and we are *"of the same mind in the Lord"* (4:2). When we step out of self and into Christ, we find joy. Conversely, when we step out of our *position* in Christ and strive in our own strength, we lose our joy. When we attempt to *think* our way out of and around the problem, rather than cling to the mind of Christ, we lose divine joy. To be "in the Lord" is to be in "a sphere of spiritual experience wherein lie unusual resources of strength and unusual expectation of behavior."[9] If we are not standing steadfast "in the

Lord", we will not be joyful. A bit of bumper sticker theology advises, "God loves everyone, but probably prefers 'fruits of the spirit over religious nuts!'"

7. Joy – the Sound that Jesus is King. Joy results from the happy news that Jesus is alive (Acts 2:14-15, 25-28). Our King, though now reigning in exile, still exerts influence on events on the earth. He maintains a presence here in the earth through the office of the invisible Holy Ghost. And He communicates with his bride-partner, the Church. One day, He will return. One day, we will rule and reign with Him. One day, the kingdoms of this world will become the Kingdom of our Lord. Until then, we have the assurance that heaven's economy is not affected by some banking crisis on the earth. We have the certainty that God will take care of us; that His sovereign reach extends into this war-torn, divided planet, plagued with heartache and disease. There is another world that is not war-torn, where the government is sure and the throne secure. There is no sickness or disease, no sorrow or crying, no death or dying. From such a world, we borrow victory and import it into our world.

8. Joy – the Sound of a Spirit-filled Church. In Acts 2, with the city full of pilgrims for the Feast of Pentecost, we might have expected the disciples to fear for their lives. Their Messiah was dead – crucified. The same leaders that had demanded His death were now leading yet another major religious festival and were no less hostile to the things he had preached. It was as if His life was unnoticed, His death a non-event, His disciples a marginal faction. God had come to the planet, only to be rejected by His own – and amazingly, to have life go on as usual. Those who had demanded the death of Jesus certainly would tolerate no more trouble from His followers!

When the day of Pentecost was fully come, with a city full of international visitors, deeply religious folks, a sound from heaven rocked the city. Fire flashed across and flooded into the upper room.

Language barriers were broken. Into the streets, these disciples rumbled with the sounds of joy. They would not hide. They would not cower. They had fresh news from heaven, brought by the Holy Spirit. God would not allow Israel or for that matter, the earth, to go on dismissing his Son. Not only was Jesus not dead, the Spirit witnessed that He had been received into heaven itself (Acts 2:3-36; Hebrews 8:1; 9:11-12, 14-15, 24-28), and had completed the mission of reconciling man to God (Romans 5:10; 2 Corinthians 5:18). Most astounding of all, He had been inaugurated as the King of the earth, and enthroned on David's throne in exile. He will rule from heaven for a season. And He will certainly return to the earth (Acts 1:11). Meanwhile, we are to serve as undercover operatives of His invisible in-breaking Kingdom. We are to be agents of the rejected-but-reigning King, serving as ambassadors to this world in which we are pilgrims. Our King is alive and is coming again. Joy is the sound of our subversive counter kingdom, even now present in the earth.

9. Joy – the Sound of the Roaring Lamb. What is subversive joy? It is the sound of the roaring Lamb! It is Stephen, seeing Jesus as the stones fell on him (Acts 7:56-60) and crying out. It is Paul and Silas, beaten and imprisoned in Philippi, who rather than react with anger, and with threats, with an immediate assertion of their rights, sang at midnight, and God visited the jail-house. This is subversive joy. How could they be happy? How could they sing? Suddenly an earthquake unshackled them, broke off the stocks and bonds, and opened the doors of the prison. It was the finger of God. They were free. Their joy did not follow the display of God's intruding power. Joy led the way!

"Weeping may endure for a night, but joy comes in the morning" (Psalm 30:5). Barnes' notes on the Bible indicates, "The word here rendered *endure* means properly *to lodge, to sojourn,* as one does for a little time. The idea is that weeping is like a stranger – a wayfaring

person – who lodges for a night only." Whatever sorrow there is for the believer, it is only temporary.[10] Joy leads the way to the morning. James says we should count it as "pure joy" when we fall into divers trials, literally "multi-colored" trials (James 1:2-3). The needy state itself is only God's opportunity. In such times your faith develops perseverance. You only grow stronger.

10. Joy – the Sound of Christians in a War Zone. "Joy runs deeper than despair," said Corrie ten Boom.[11] Robert E. Lee, the great Confederate General, declared amazingly, "I don't see how we could have an army without music." Both the Union and the South had bands. About four million dollars a year was invested in the musicians. At times, in the evenings, when the battle had died down, both sides listened to band music, sometimes from across the lines. There are reports of their blending their music together. In the middle of the Civil War, there were as many as 618 bands, one musician in service for every 41 soldiers. When the battle raged, at its most intense moments, the generals instructed the bands to play. And music inspired the men to fight. At times, the bands themselves seemed to be warring with one another.

The Benefits of Joy

A group of Maryland researchers discovered that victims of heart disease were 40 percent less likely to laugh, even in obviously humorous situations, than those with healthy hearts.[12] One 13 year study of people struggling with major depression found that their risk of a heart attack was 450 percent higher than those with no depression.[13] And their chances of dying from a heart attack were increased by 400 percent.[14] Depression aggravated their medical condition.

1. Joy Improves Your Health.
  • Laughter relaxes the whole body. A good, hearty laugh relieves physical tension and stress, leaving your muscles re-

laxed for up to 45 minutes after.

- Laughter boosts the immune system. Laughter decreases stress hormones and increases immune cells and infection-fighting antibodies, thus improving your resistance to disease.
- Laughter triggers the release of endorphins, the body's natural feel-good chemicals. Endorphins promote an overall sense of well-being and can even temporarily relieve pain.
- Laughter protects the heart. Laughter improves the function of blood vessels and increases blood flow, which can help protect you against a heart attack and other cardiovascular problems.[15]

One report says, "Laughter moves lymph fluid around your body simply by the convulsions you experience during the process of laughing…it boosts immune system function…your lymph system doesn't have a separate pump." Laughter is God's way "to properly circulate lymph fluid so that your immune system can carry out its natural functions."

There is more – "laughter increases oxygenation of your body at both the cellular and organ level." And this – "Oxygen is one of the primary catalysts for biological energy…an element of intracellular energy that's absolutely necessary to sustain human life." Cancer cells thrive in the absence of adequate oxygen, and are destroyed in its presence.[16] Laugh. Eighty-three percent of patients in one study believed that laughter helped them get through the difficult days of illness. The impact of laughter on health is so compelling that some hospitals have hired clowns. The Big Apple Circus Clown Care Unit was initiated in 1986, and has spawned many comparable clown units across the U.S. and around the world.[17]

An 11-year-old boy, doused with gasoline and set on fire by an older boy, was brought to a hospital with a clown program, still conscious, but in terrible pain. Half his body had major burns. He was taken into surgery immediately, and accompanying the surgical team, was the hospital clown. As the surgeon started slicing away dead tissue, the clown started telling the boy funny stories. He promised circus tickets, made scarves appear and disappear, anything to distract him from his pain. Suddenly, the boy was laughing. He was facing death and in dreadful pain – laughing. It made the experience bearable.

Some hospitals now provide a "humor cart" loaded with CDs and DVDs, sources of humor. In one study, patients were given serious dramatic movies for entertainment, another group watched comedies. Those who watched comedies requested 61 percent less minor pain medication, aspirin and or mild tranquilizers for two days following their watching the movie. Those who could choose movies that fit their humor profile had even more dramatic results, reporting fewer major pain episodes.

2. Humor Affects Your Closest Relationships. Now a software analysis package called SMILE[18] provides a personalized humor prescription as a part of the healing regiment. Humor-type therapies, called psychosocial interventions, reduce hospital stays by an average of 2.4 days. The mind heals the body. That connection showed up 79 percent of the time, usually creating a shorter hospital stay. Reduction of medical complications was also a major factor. Patients used less pain and nausea medication.

Dr. James Walsh pioneered the humor and medicine movement. Recent research in psycho-neuro-immunology has confirmed his intuition. It may not be so much what laughter does, but what it prevents, namely, the disruption in the production of neurotransmitters, hormones and other substances associated with stress and negative emotion that interfere with the healing process. It speeds up post-surgical healing and lowers blood cortisol levels, which then frees the Natural Killer cells to do their work.[19]

One study, covering subjects over a 60-year period, demonstrates a connection between an individual's smile intensity and the divorce rate. The less intense the smile, the greater likelihood there was of a divorce. Those who smile may have a more positive outlook on life. They also live longer. Smiles are, of course, spontaneous. However, even when patients were told to smile, to really smile, their brains registered subjective enjoyment associated with the spontaneous smile. Even a forced smile may have positive benefits.[20] God created us to smile. Peace starts with a smile.

The name Isaac, the son of Abraham, means *laughter.* And it was Isaac that unstopped the wells that the enemies had plugged up. Laughter opens the wells causing the springs to flow again. It transforms behavior, people and places, into well watered gardens. Loma Linda University Medical Center discovered, through the work of Dr. Lee Berk, that indeed, laughter boosts the immune system and reduces dangerous hormones.

In one control group, the exposure to a funny video saw their hormone level of cortisol fall an amazing 39 percent. Adrenaline (epinephrine) levels fell 70 percent. Endorphin levels rose by 27 percent – so they felt better. More importantly, the level of the so-called "youth hormone" which affects growth and healing, skyrocketed by 87 percent.[21] Berk's work indicates additional corollary benefits. *Immunoglobulin A* is increased, protecting against respiratory tract infections. Gamma interferon accelerates, raising the defense against viruses. B cells produce antibodies that go after harmful bacteria.

The average adult laughs 25 times a day. The average child – 400 times a day.[22] *"Except you become as a little child, you will not enter the kingdom."* There is a dimension of kingdom living, here and now that we can only know – as *children* of God.

3. Joy Keeps Your Disposition Positive. The Greek word for joy is a call to "cheer up!" The needs that drive us to prayer are not to deter our joy – an utterly irrational idea. But that is the nature of Kingdom joy. It is subversive, incongruent with our worldly situation, against the norm. Circumstances suggest we should be sad and sullen, but instead we celebrate. This is Paul and Silas in jail, in stocks and bonds, their backs bleeding - they should have been weeping. Instead of being angry and retaliatory, they are having a party. This is a matter of days after the departure of Jesus, only seven weeks after the crucifixion. They might have been in mourning. Instead, they were celebrating like intoxicated, party people. They had heard news from another world that had altered their attitude – Jesus was alive, accepted and enthroned in heaven. Webb Garrison says, "Faith is positive, enriching life in the here and now. Doubt is negative, robbing life of glow and meaning."[23]

4. Joy Draws on Deep Resources. The word *rejoice* is in the present imperative adding intensity. It means, *"Keep on rejoicing!"*[24] Don't stop. Joy is to be a constant in our lives. Happiness and joy are not the same. Happiness is drawn from life's daily circumstances. Happiness lives off the rain and the sunshine. Its condition is dictated by circumstances, day by day. But joy draws water from deep springs when the cistern is dry. Joy drives water to the dry surface. We draw deeply on a source that is not tempered by droughts and floods. Joy, imported joy, feeds happiness. Joy is the mark of a deep person. It refuses to be superficial. Joy is evidence that we ourselves believe that we will be heard when we pray. And when the answer comes it is time to "tell some-

Key Principle

Attitude is an intriguing aeronautical term. Airplanes take off, fly 'nose up'. Whenever the nose is down it indicates a bad attitude and it is necessary to make an 'attitude adjustment'. You never want to be on an airplane with a bad attitude.

body!" Such stories fuel faith in others, even our small victories. Share joy.

5. Joy Keeps Your Nose Up. *Attitude* is an intriguing aeronautical term. It seems odd to speak of an aircraft's *attitude*. Airplanes take off, fly and land in a 'nose up' position. Whenever the nose is down, the aircraft is said to have a 'bad attitude.' Planes with a bad attitude crash unless the pilot can make an 'attitude adjustment.' You never want to be on an airplane with a bad attitude. Do you have a 'nose-up' attitude or a 'nose-down' attitude? The clearest indication that you and I are on a crash course with our spiritual lives is when we are found with a *bad attitude*. Nose down. Depressed. Full of anxiety. Under pressure. Weighted down by life's cares.

E. Stanley Jones, the great Christian leader commented,

Many live in dread of what is coming. Why should we? The unknown puts adventure into life. It gives us something to sharpen our souls on. The unexpected around the corner gives us a sense of anticipation and surprise. Thank God for the unknown future. If we saw all good things which are coming to us, we would sit down and degenerate. If we saw all the evil things, we would be paralyzed. How merciful God is to lift the curtain today; and as we get strength today to meet tomorrow, then to lift the curtain on the morrow. He is a considerate God.[25]

Joy, not an emotion, but an act of the will, is the attitude corrector that God uses - rejoice. *"Rejoice – in the Lord! Always."* Though we might be tempted, we should never put a question mark where God has put a period. *"Rejoice. Always."* This is not joy out of our emotional disposition, the reflection of our changeable feelings. This is the discipline of joy. It is joy borrowed from heaven. It is joy seized by the saved soul as he stands in the mouth of the empty tomb. It is imported joy from heaven's throne. It is 'nose up' joy, a heavenward view. It is joy that comes as a result of the sweet whispering of Jesus, the lover of our soul. We have gotten news again, *"The Lord is at hand."*

6. Joy Defies the Enemy. Winston Churchill used to say, "Nothing in life is so exhilarating as to be shot at without result."[26] After the bullets have flown, after the thunder has ceased, after the Evil One has tempted us unsuccessfully, we are exhilarated. We have been 'shot at' without result. During the Civil War, it took "a man's weight in lead to kill a single enemy in battle."[27] One Union ammunitions expert calculated that to wound a Confederate "required 240 pounds of powder and 900 pounds of lead." A lot of lead never found its mark. It was the atmosphere that was deadly.[28]

When Nehemiah began to rebuild the wall, Sanballat and Tobiah began to hurl words and threats. The tension intensified. The bullying was intended to stress the builders – and it did. They *"conspired to come together to come and attack Jerusalem [the fortress of peace], and bring confusion"* (Nehemiah 4:8). Prayer was intensified. A watch was set in place. There were bad-news messengers who carried the deadly warnings from the enemy and planted them among the workers, paralyzing them with fear, *"They told us ten times, 'From wherever place you turn, they will be upon us'"* (Nehemiah 4:12). Nehemiah was not careless. He took precautions, pairing "prayer" (watchers) warriors with workers. But he refused to allow the work to be stopped by fear.

There were at least five escalating phases to the conflict. But in the end, there was never an attack. Not one arrow was shot. It was all huff and puff. The work was finished. The wall was joined together. The gates were set in place. The city had been restored. Nehemiah would exhort, *"The joy of the Lord is our strength"* (Nehemiah 8:10).

7. Joy is Natural. Animals and children play instinctively. Life was meant to have playtimes! We, as adults, allow life's troubles to crowd out play. Next to love and faith, humor – or joy – is God's great gift. It relaxes. It cleanses and inspires. It is the savor of life itself. Dr. Glenn Clark, a great prayer leader noted, "Joy binds man to God and gives him atonement."[29] This is "joy, born of certainty of the greatest realities, that man is forever united to all that is good, and forever regenerated…joy synchronizes with the answer."[30]

An Island of Joy

North Platte, Nebraska is a relatively sleepy little mid-western town with a population of only some 20,000. It sits just north of I-80. It isn't Lincoln or Omaha. Few today would know its significance. In the days before the interstate, North Platte was big. It was a railroad town. During WWII, it seemed that half the armed forces passed through the little Nebraska town, coming or going. "Every day from 1942 to 1945, as many as 10,000 servicemen and women came through North Platte on the troop trains on their way to war." The total? – Six million? Eight million? No one knows. But patriotism ran deep in and around North Platte, and in nearby little towns like Elk Creek, Buffalo Grove, Lodgepole and Dry Valley. Those hardy Midwesterners met every train, fed every sailor and soldier, and never collected a dime from anyone.

What a model for the church! The North Platte people learned that a Nebraska National Guard unit was being activated and would travel right through their town. One resident recalled, "Lordy, everybody that had anybody that knew anybody that was in the service was down at that station with cookies and candy and what have you." The whole town waited all day. The train came in late, but it was not the Nebraska Guard, but the Kansas Guard. In the end, it didn't matter. They gave their gifts to the Kansas boys along with hugs and tears, and meeting the troop trains in North Platte never stopped.

The effort involved some 120 little towns as far away as 200 miles. "They came with baskets of food!" There were birthday cakes. Sweets. Chicken. Pheasants. Coffee. Relish. An eleven-year-old boy showed up regularly at the Nebraska cattle auction. He would auction the shirt off his back to the highest bidder and use the proceeds to buy a beef for the soldiers. Most of the time, he got his shirt back and left with a donation for the troops. Officers and fresh recruits both got the same treatment. Those who lost loved ones in the war came to serve, never letting a soldier know the tenderness of their own heart. At times, some sat down at the piano and the whole room lit up in song. North Platte was an island of joy in the middle of a nation at war. Joy. Sacrificial joy.

The church ought to be a little like the folks of North Platte. It should be a place where people on their way to an unknown fate loaded with potential danger could hear the music, get a cup of coffee and sense a bit of caring love.[31] What if we parked in an intersection full of people in transition, and offered prayer wrapped in care? What if we found the location where a stream of hurting people moved through our town, and we discovered a way to demonstrate the love of God?

Prayer should never be used solely as a personal and private benefit. It ought to be given away – and wrapped in joy.

REVIEW It

1. Helen Keller said joy was like _____.
2. Samuel Shoemaker said, "The surest sign of a Christian is not faith, or even _____, but joy."
3. Joy is _____ against the norm, defiant of the world's conditions and moods.
4. Life was meant to have _____.
5. There is a difference between joy and _____.

TALK About It

1. Talk about the idea of keeping your 'nose up.'
2. What is meant by the idea of subversive joy?

3. In what way are we to be dressed for joy?

4. Talk about the glimpse into heaven, Revelation 4-5, in the context of the depressing condition of the church (2-3), and the unfolding geopolitical scene (6).

5. Have you ever known a fellow-believer who seemed to live in a state of grace and peace, a kind of bubble, when an earthly reality check called for tears and tension, among so-called normal people? Who was it – and what do you most remember about him or her?

Endnotes

1. Barney Warren. *Joy Unspeakable* (Evening Light Songs, Faith Publishing House, 1949, edited 1987, 88); also: (The Gospel Trumpet Company, Select Hymns, 1911), 183. (Written in 1900).

2. Bruce Main, *Spotting the Sacred: Noticing God in the Most Unlikely Places* (Grand Rapids, MI: Baker Book House, 2006).

3. Martin H. Manser, *The Westminster Collection Of Christian Quotations* (Westminster: John Knox Press, 2001), 214.4.

4. Richard Wurmbrand, *Tortured for Christ, 30th Anniversary Edition* (Bartlesville, OK: Living Sacrifice Book Company, 1998), 63.

5. P. Douglas Small, *Entertaining God* (Kannapolis, NC: Alive Publications, 1992, 2009).

6. See: Hope, Bob; Ann T. Keene, author: www.anb.org/articles/18/18-03790-print.html. Also see Hope's memoirs *I Never Left Home* (1944); William Robert Faith, *Bob Hope: A Life in Comedy* (2003).

7. Wesley Duewel, *Touch the World Through Prayer* (Zondervan, 1986), 141.

8. Quoted by Bill Bright, *Discover the Real Jesus* (Bright Media Foundation, 2004), 47.

9. Stuart Briscoe. *Bound for Joy* (Glendale, CA: Gospel Light; 1975), 133.

10. Albert Barnes, *Barnes' Notes on the Old and New Testaments, Psalms* (1983).

11. Dennis Cory, *Devotions for the Wounded Heart* (Bloomington, IN: WestBow Press, A Division of Thomas Nelson, 2011), 125.

12. An excerpt from *Christian Clippings*, December, 2001, 18. (Source: *Have a Good Day*, Tyndale House Publishers. March, 2001).

13. Harold George Koenig, Michael E. McCullough, David B. Larson

Pratt, *Handbook of Religion and Health,* 1996, p. 119; As part of a survey of the Baltimore Epidemiologic Catchment Area funded by the NIMH, Pratt et al. (1996) conducted a 13-year prospective study of 1551 subjects. See also: Pamela S. Douglas, *Cardiovascular Health and Disease in Women; Mental Health in Public Health: The Next 100 Years,* 194; For example, a 13-year prospective study showed a 4.5 times greater risk of a heart attack among those with major depression (Pratt et al., 1996), and in another study mortality was 4 times higher among depressed heart attack patients.

14. Don Colbert, *Deadly Emotions: Understand the Mind-Body-Spirit Connection That Can Heal Or Destroy You* (Nashville, TN: Thomas Nelson, 2006), 64.

15. www.helpguide.org/life/humor_laughter_health.htm.

16. Excerpted from, Mike Adams, *The Five Habits of Health Transformation* (Truth Publication International, 2006). The book covers the five most effective, yet effortless strategies for enhancing health. Written for busy people, it explains how to get the greatest health results possible with the least investment in time, money or effort. Learn more: www.naturalnews.com/007551.html#ixzz1LJiYtwhh.

17. An example is the Fondation Theodora in France.

18. The acronym SMILE stands for – "Subjective Multidimensional Interactive Laughter Evaluation."

19. *American Association for Therapeutic Humor Newsletter* (June, 1999). See also: http://www.nurseslearning.com/courses/nrp/NRPCX-W0009/html/body.humor.page6.htm. Also see: *The Hospital Clown,* by Shobhana Schwebke "Shobi Dobi". The Theodora Foundation operates in more than 30 hospitals in Switzerland and on four continents, as well as for the L'association Le Rire Médecin in France. Other organizations following this model include: Die Clown Doktoren (Germany), Doctor Clown (England), Clown-doctors (Scotland), l'Association Docteur Clown (Lyon, France), Clown Docs (St Louis, Missouri), Clowns on Rounds (Upper State New York), Doutores da Alegria (Brazil), Fools for Health (Windsor, Ontario), and Doc Willikers (Vancouver, BC).

Within the body's ecosystem, Natural Killer (NK) cells police tumors and infected cells, sparing healthy cells. They eliminate their targets, and only their targets, in hours after their discovery. Scientists are now learning how these killers target cancer, for example. They are cousins to the T cells, and special agents of the immune system. NK cells patrol the body and mark cancer or infected cells. Once identified, these sick cells are destroyed in minutes by a mechanism known as cytotoxicity. Read more: https://www.sciencedaily.com/terms/natural_killer_cell.htm; https://www.youtube.com/watch?v=HNP1EAYLhOs

20. www.psychologytoday.com/blog/humor-sapiens/201104/the-long-lasting-effect-smile

21. Colbert, 179.

22. Ibid, 183.

23. Webb Garrison. Quoted by J. Maurus, Just a Moment Please (Bombay: St. Paul Society, 1988), 204. See also: Webb Garrison Quote: publicquotes.com/quote/25355/faith-is-positive-enriching-life-in-the-here-and-now.html.

24. John Walvoord. *Philippians: Triumph in Christ* (Moody Press: Chicago; 1971), 105.

25. Garrison.

26. Alan Axelrod, *Winston Churchill, CEO: 25 Lessons for Bold Business Leaders* (New York: Sterling Publishing Company, 2009), 27.

27. Burke Davis, *The Civil War – Strange and Fascinating Facts* (New York: Wings Books, a division of Random House Value Publishing; 1996; Previously published as, Our Incredible Civil War by Holt, Rinehart and Winston; 1960), 135.

28. Ibid.

29. Glenn Clark, The Soul's Sincere Desire (Macalester Park Publishing Company, 1988), 76.

30. Ibid.

31. Charles Kuralt, "On the Road with Charles Kuralt," *American Names* (New York: Fawcett Gold Metal; 1985), 18-23.

REVIEW It Answers

1. Fire
2. Love
3. Subversive
4. Play times
5. Happiness

My soul in sad exile was out on life's sea,
So burdened with sin and distressed,
Till I heard a sweet voice, saying,
"Make Me your choice;"
And I entered the Haven of Rest!
I yielded myself to His tender embrace,
In faith taking hold of the Word,
My fetters fell off, and I anchored my soul;
The Haven of Rest is my Lord.
The song of my soul, since the Lord made me whole,
Has been the old story so blest,
Of Jesus, Who'll save whosoever will have
A home in the Haven of Rest.
How precious the thought that we all may recline,
Like John, the belovèd so blest,
On Jesus' strong arm, where no tempest can harm,
Secure in the Haven of Rest.
O come to the Savior, He patiently waits
To save by His power divine;
Come, anchor your soul in the Haven of Rest,
And say, "My Belovèd is mine."

Refrain
I've anchored my soul in the Haven of Rest,
I'll sail the wide seas no more;
The tempest may sweep over wild, stormy, deep,
In Jesus I'm safe evermore.[1]

CHAPTER SIX
Step Three: Be Gentle to All Men

Let your gentleness be known to all men!

Perspective: "Gentle" may not be the best translation. The word here is one that is difficult to translate. It means steadiness, moderation, graciousness, poise; all in the middle of some needy state. The ability to remain under the load, to act and not react, is an extraordinary evidence of another power working in our lives. This is the essence of a quality Christ-like witness: gentleness and graciousness. We arrive here only by practicing the radical extremes of this passage. Rejoice always; be gracious to all men; don't worry about anything; give thanks in the face of everything; pray about all your needs. These are radical ideas. The result is persistent joy, grace under fire, and militant peace. What a witness.

In the Christmas season of 1917, European landscapes, normally beautified by snow, were darkened with the residue of black powder from war. Americans and Germans were hunkered down in their respective trenches with a strip of barbed wire, called No Man's Land, between them. The exchange of fire was intense. A young German had bravely ventured into the treacherous zone between the trenches and laid badly wounded. Despite the intensity of the bombardments, the sound of his screams reverberated on both sides. When the shelling grew quiet, even his whimpers could be clearly heard. He became the symbol of the inevitable and potential fate of every man. For hours, his torture continued, until a young American soldier, acting independently, did what no one else would do. He crawled from the safety of the allied trench and slithered his way toward the wounded enemy. His colleagues ceased fire to keep from wounding him. A German officer realized what was happening and also ordered a cease fire. From both sides, men watched him wiggle his way under the sharp barbs of wire until he reached the wounded German. Those present recalled the moment as "a weird and tense silence." Cutting his enemy free, and disentangling the sharp barbs, he stood up with his wounded adversary in his arms. Then he walked straight toward the German trenches. Without a word, he placed him in the arms of his buddies and turned to return to the American trench, as if the rules of war had been for a moment suspended. As he turned, a hand on his shoulder drew him back. He was face to face with a German officer decorated with an Iron Cross, their highest honor for bravery. The officer tore the Iron Cross from his uniform and pinned it on the American. Then he released him to walk back across No Man's Land to his place of battle and the madness of war resumed.[2]

The Terms

In the midst of needs, we are to let our *moderation* (Philippians 4:5, KJV) be known. It can mean *forbearance*, a disposition of *gentleness*.[3] An even better translation would be *steady* or *gracious*. It is the idea of keeping our poise under pressure, of staying cool under fire, of acting and not reacting. Wycliffe translates the word as *patience*, Tyndale as *softness*, perhaps implying a tenderness toward others even when we are in the midst of pain ourselves.

The meaning of the word is difficult to convey. It also can mean to be *considerate*. It is a "remembrance of others that forgets self." This "selfless man" is as firm as a rock on moral principle, but as soft as a feather in his relationship with others. Such a balance between uncompromising truth and unconditional love is perfection in a true Christian. Holding tightly to truth, we can become tough, hard and critical, arrogant and insensitive. Holding exclusively to love, we are morally undefined and fuzzy on principle. The perfect poise implied here balances love and truth. It is a picture of the yielding of personal rights without violating principle.[4] This steadfast *moderation* is the basis of our witness before a watching world.

A denominational evangelism leader tapped a prayer trainer on the shoulder, gave him a wink and pulled him aside. "I think this prayer thing is a great idea, but I'm afraid it might get out of hand...people could get so caught up in praying they wouldn't do anything."[5]

Paul would have been shocked by such a view of prayer. Our prayerful dependence on God as we request of Him, and our witness before men are connected to evangelism. Before the answer comes, we exhibit faith and joy, poise and peace. And when the answer comes, it is an opportunity to testify of the loving God who answers prayer.

> **Key Principle**
>
> The heart of the passage is the *Great Exchange*. We give God our troubles and He agrees to hear and meet our needs. In exchange for such a wonderful deal, we agree to make "happy sounds." To praise Him. Our poise is the evidence of our faith.

Tender Tenaciousness – Staying Sweet

Someone has said, "A truly happy person is the one who can enjoy the scenery on a detour."[6] This passage calls for us to exude a "sweet reasonableness"[7] – in the place of the demands we might make on others.[8] One translation renders the same word clemency.[9]

"Let your graciousness, your reasonableness be known" to all men. It is to be our personal calling card. Noisy moderate Christians – are to be noticed by everyone. The idea is obviously contradictory. Being simultaneously moderate and noisy doesn't seem congruent. Yet, under pressure and in the face of unmet or even some potentially devastating outcome, we remain steady. We keep our poise. We exhibit joy and grace.

The Test – Singing at Exam Time

The heart of the passage is the *Great Exchange* offered by God. We give Him our troubles and He agrees to hear and meet our needs. In exchange for such a wonderful deal, we agree to make "happy sounds." To praise Him. To rejoice – that He is there to hear and answer, whatever the outcome. Our poise, when others might crack under such pressure, is the evidence of our faith. And that kind of faith gets rewarded with answers. Others come to know Him by watching us over some season of time, that we will endure this storm as we did the last one – generally gracious and cool under pressure, poised and confident in our God, exhibiting joy and expressing thanks to God. Our behavior is predictable, even if it also approaches the miraculous. We are singing while taking our exams – and we may not even know the answers. But He does.

The Treasures – Living out of Heaven's Plenty

Petitions often involve our requests for God to change circumstances, to intervene, to supply a need, to open a door, to bring heaven's resources to bear on some personal matter. But they are to be offered by a joyful and gracious soul that refuses to allow the very real earthly and temporal need not to dictate our demeanor. Heaven's certainties and its treasure troves are the values to which our heart is attuned. We may live *in* a world of *need,* but we live *out of* a world of *provision.* Prayer is not something we start doing after a problem comes; it is something we do before and keep doing after a problem comes.[10] We pray *"in season and out"* of season (2 Timothy 4:2).

Taking Radical Action

The pathway to calm in the middle of a storm is only found in the radical behaviors suggested by this passage. Only extreme Christians get here. Average Christians sadly live joyless lives that are less than an adequate witness to the triumphant Lamb turned Lion. The radical action plan of Paul demands that we disconnect the inner "fear alarm" and turn on the music of joy. Stop counting problems. Start being verbally grateful for every little thing. John Wayne used to say, "Courage is being scared to death but saddling up anyway."

Joy and peace express an inner confidence in the ultimate triumph of God in any matter. They are the companions of faith, evidence of effervescent hope, a bubbling certainty that God's word and promises are true, his guarantees as good as gold. It is this inner joy and peace that allows us to be gentle, to retain our poise under pressure. When we are stressed and stretched beyond common levels of endurance, we remain gracious and gentle by the strength of this supernatural joy and peace. The Lord is near people with such dispositions, along with an amazing spiritual equilibrium. Prayer has invited him. But this is not where the average believer lives. Such notions seem extreme. And this passage is loaded with radical extremes.

A – Act in Accord with the Radical Extremes. ALWAYS. What extremes! We rejoice – sometimes. Offer gentleness – to a selected few. Worry – too often. Give thanks – too little. Pray about some things.

B – Be Reassured by Past Experiences. *"Let your moderation be made known"* – the word *known* refers to knowledge acquired by experience.[11] Poise under pressure is possible because God has delivered us in the past, and we believe that He will hear us now. When problems come, perhaps unconsciously, we ask others to do what only God can do. Stressed people stress others. Experience should temper that. Paul urges us here, to not allow needs to motivate us to lay unduly rigid and unreasonable expectations on others.

Knowing God will hear us gives us the quiet confidence to be a calming influence, rather than an agitating agent. We are to be gentle and gracious. We are to treat others with lenience. We are not to demand from others what is unreasonable. And we are to be satisfied, even when we have received less than what may be due to us. These are extraordinarily gracious standards.

With pressures pushing and pulling at us, our loss of balance causes us to push and pull at others. We react, rather than act. We may be anything but gentle. We are less than temperate – we may boil over. This is exactly the opposite of Paul's formula here. Someone cryptically said, "If you can't be kind, at least have the decency to be vague." Warren Buffet reminds us, "You don't have to be first. The second mouse gets the cheese."[12]

C – Choose the Right Examples. These ideas center on the quality of our Christian witness – joy and poise under pressure. Steadiness under fire. Never so pressured that we stop making happy sounds. Poised, but not so subdued that we have stopped singing. By grace, we remain steady, assuming an even disposition, an even keel, inner calmness through whatever storm we may be traveling. Even when we have pain, we don't have to be one.

In truth, this is, by modern terms, irrational – and it is a life foreign to many Christians. We resonate with the pressures of this world and lose the melody of heaven. We switch songs and moods. We mirror this world in any present moment. Great men of Scripture stayed on heaven's script. Noah kept building his ark and Abraham kept searching for his city. Moses kept leading through the wilderness. David kept securing this throne. Nehemiah kept building his wall. And Jesus kept heading for the cross, confident of what was beyond it.

With friends and family watching, you and I are to remain steady under fire. We broadcast our moderation to everyone. All see the sturdy and steady state of our soul despite the crisis. Someone said, "You can learn a lot about a person by how he handles three things – a rainy day, lost luggage, and tangled Christmas lights."[13]

D – Deploy Your Gyroscope. My Dad was in the Navy serving in the Pacific in World War II. The huge ships on which he served fascinate me. They defy the liquid waves. The stability of an aircraft carrier allows a jet to take off and land on its deck. The variance allowed for such a maneuver is minute.

How can a ship remain so steady riding the unstable liquid sea? In its hull is a huge gyroscope. The giant energy engine has an input axis that fields the ocean's energy. It also has a spin axis that diffuses destabilizing energy, allowing the output axis to remain perpendicular. In effect, with its spin axis, it absorbs and diffuses energy, maintaining equilibrium. It exudes energy and thereby diffuses the impact of the ocean's vigorously surging waves that would otherwise destabilize the ship. In doing so, it creates its own energy field.

You and I are to maintain our poise and moderation. We are to be gracious and gentle on choppy and stormy seas. We can do this only by engaging in extremes. Rejoice – *always*. Sing. *Refuse* to worry – *ever*. Thank God *all the time*. Pray about *everything*. And the Holy Spirit, like an inner gyroscope, helps us diffuse the world's destabilizing negative energy, effectively creating an alternative energy field when counter forces would unsteady us.

E – Engage the Moment. Jesus lived in the moment. He managed to contain the negative energy of one experience in its place, without allowing it to flow into the next moment and color His outlook. He went through a storm on the Sea of Galilee and arrived safely on the shore, only to meet a man with a storm inside his whole being – one did not color the other, He lived in the moment (Matthew 8:28). He was teaching in a crowded house, only to have the roof above Him open up to allow a paralytic to be lowered down creating a disruption – he healed the man, using the spontaneous intrusion He lived in the moment (Mark 2:1-5). Teaching again, His message was interrupted with a frantic request by a ruler whose daughter had died. In route to reach the dead girl, He was thronged and touched by a woman, unclean by Mosaic standards, with a physical condition called "an issue of blood" (an unstoppable hemorrhage) – through it all, He lived in the moment (Matthew 9:14, 18, 20f).

In need of solitude and rest, He was haunted by hungry crowds. His disciples carried the weariness of ministry into the wilderness with them; they did not live in the moment. They pleaded with Him to send the needy crowd away (Matthew 14:15). But Jesus refused to send them away hungry. He took charge, broke bread and fed them – living in the moment. After He had read from the scroll of Isaiah, the people from His own synagogue led him to the cliff overlooking the city, intending to end His life. He was insane, they believed. Blasphemous. They were so close to Him, they could not see Him. They could not rejoice that from their own midst had

Key Principle

We maintain our poise by engaging in extremes. Rejoice – *always.* Sing. *Refuse* to worry – *ever.* Thanks God *all the time.* Prayer about *everything.* And the Holy Spirit effectively creates an alternative energy field.

emerged the Messiah. They were overwrought, but He calmly walked away, passing through their midst (Luke 4:14-30). This ability to diffuse the negative influences and *energy of the world* and of Satan's push-pull strategies is critical to balance. Our obedient action invites the Holy Spirit to work in and around our lives to counteract the negative pressures.

F – Focus on Heaven's Victory. In our rejoicing, we pull down heaven's victory. We express it. We verbalize it. We declaratively own it. Before the watching world, we are, by grace, to appear rock solid, moderate, gracious and gentle. *"The Lord is near!"* We are acting as if His return were *imminent,* any moment. We are acting as if His presence were *immediate,* intimately with us. This is the heart of the passage, the place where it becomes dynamically alive. We have joy, poise, and a sense of His nearness – three positives. Let's examine the moving parts of the passage.

First, the prohibition – *don't worry.* That prohibition insinuates that waters ahead may be infested with alligators and the land loaded with beastly predators. The world is full of dangers. The devil is real and warfare against believers is a palpable reality. Yet the advice of Paul is *"don't worry!"* Prohibitions are difficult! Told not to think about a certain thing, that *thing* is precisely the thing about which we think. Paul offsets the prohibition with three positive actions. First of all, before anything else – *pray.* Second, be *supple* – pliable, bendable, flexible. Third, *be thankful.* Then, detail your problem in prayer, asking for God's intervention!

Susan is the name Charles Swindoll gave her. Knocking at her door was a strange man, asking if a certain person lived in her complex. Susan said "No" and thought nothing more of it. Moments later, there was another knock. This time, the same man forced his way into her apartment. His earlier knock assured him she was alone. After surveying the building, he returned, intending to rape her. An incredible serenity swept over Susan. It was the militant peace of God. With extraordinary personal composure, she declared to the assailant that she was a Christian, serving the ever present and sovereign God, and nothing was going to happen that was not according to His will. Susan declared her belief that God had a plan for her life, and then she asked her intruder, "Has anyone every told you that God has a plan for your life?"

Stunned, he said, "No." Susan proceeded to invite him to sit down next to her and she calmly outlined the love of God to the man. With his weapon on the table in front of them, she prayed with him to receive Christ. He thanked her, arose and left her apartment. Suddenly, as quickly as he left, panic swept her soul. And she realized how close to death she had come. But, in the moments that mattered, God's presence brought the bubble of peace that allowed the perfect poise and confidence to turn the situation. One life was spared. One soul was saved.

REVIEW It

1. Let your _____, _____, and _____ be made known to all men.
2. We live in a world of need, and out of a world of _____.
3. We are to _____ always.
4. Joy and peace express our inner confidence in the ultimate _____ of God.
5. "The Lord is at hand" can mean – His coming is _____ or His presence is immediate.

TALK About It

1. Talk about the various meanings of the word *moderation*.
2. Explore the importance of 'poise' before a watching world where 'problems' crowd in around us.

3. Discuss the tension between rejoicing and being moderate.
4. Talk about the radical extremes of the passage.
5. Why do you think we lose our spiritual balance?

End Notes

1. Henry L. Gilmour, "Haven of Rest" (Public Domain, 1890; Sunlight Songs, John R. Sweney, et al. (Philadelphia, PA: John J. Hood, 1890).
2. Alice Gray, Stories for the Heart (Gresham, OR: Vision House Publishing, 1996), 29.
3. M. R. Vincent. *Word Studies in the New Testament, Volume II* (MacDonald Publishing Company, MacDill Air Force Base, Tampa, FL), 891.
4. H. C. G. Moule. *Studies in Philippians* (Grand Rapids, MI: Kregel; 1977), 111.
5. Ronald Dunn, *Don't Just Stand There – Pray Something!* (Nashville, TN: Thomas Nelson, 1991), 17.
6. Jack Canfield, Mark Victor Hansen, Amy Newmark, *Chicken Soup for the Soul: Tough Times, Tough People – 101 Stories* (New York: Simon and Schuster, 2009), 27.
7. Kenneth Wuest. *Wuest's Word Studies, Philippians in the Greek New Testament* (Grand Rapids, MI: Eerdmans, 1942), 109.
8. John Walvoord. *Philippians: Triumph in Christ* (Moody Press: Chicago; 1971), 105.
9. Ibid.
10. Will Davis, Jr. *Pray Big* (Grand Rapids, MI: Revell, 2007), 84.
11. Wuest, 109.
12. U.S. News & World Report, "Reviews" (U.S. News Pub. Corp., 2004), Volume 136.
13. Susan Sparks, *Laugh Your Way to Grace: Reclaiming the Spiritual Power of Humor* (Woodstock, VT; SkyLight Paths Publishing, 2010), 16.

REVIEW It Answers

1. Gentleness, Moderation, Poise
2. Plenty
3. Rejoice
4. Triumph
5. Imminent

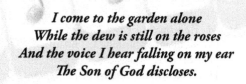

I come to the garden alone
While the dew is still on the roses
And the voice I hear falling on my ear
The Son of God discloses.

He speaks, and the sound of His voice,
Is so sweet the birds hush their singing,
And the melody that He gave to me
Within my heart is ringing.

I'd stay in the garden with Him
Though the night around me be falling,
But He bids me go; through the voice of woe
His voice to me is calling.

Refrain
And He walks with me, and He talks with me,
And He tells me I am His own;
And the joy we share as we tarry there,
None other has ever known.[1]

CHAPTER SEVEN
Step Four: Experience God's Nearness

The Lord Is at Hand!

Perspective: A sense of God's nearness will excite faith, raise confidence, reinforce the certain sense of His love – and with that, we feel that we are more than conquerors. God created man for unbroken fellowship with Him. We don't work right without that. Sometimes the static and interference of the world breaks our sense of God's nearness. At times, inner noises, the flesh creates the dissonance. And then there is the devil himself. God wants to be near us. *"Lo, I am with you always!"* Jesus declared. It is His desire. With a sense of God's presence – we are indomitable.

"Pop" Muncy was the cafeteria manager during my days at what is now Lee University. I worked for him washing pots and pans. He had been a successful pastor and a State Overseer. At times, he would wander through the work area where I and a few other students were a captive audience and hold forth on some Biblical principle. Great preachers stood behind the pulpit during our chapel services, many with advanced degrees. Pop Muncy was not lettered, but his chapel message is one I have never forgotten. Near his house in his childhood years, a large rock seemed to transform itself, taking on the shape of a monster. He called it "Booger Rock." Prior to the days of streetlights, passing that rock at night was the greatest horror of his young life. He ran past it. He refused to look at it. "Booger Rock" terrified him. On one night however, he passed that rock holding onto his father's hand. How different that experience was – there was no fear. He stared the rock down. He almost felt like daring it. The difference was his father's presence.

The Bible says the Lord, our God is *"round about His people"* (Psalm 125:2). Even his name is a *"strong tower"* (Proverbs 18:10). Deuteronomy declares, the Lord is *"as an eagle…that fluttereth over her young"* – He is above us (Deuteronomy 32:11-12). *"Underneath are the everlasting arms"* of the eternal God, our *"dwelling place"* (Deuteronomy 33:27). David declared, *"I have set the Lord always before me: because He is at my right hand, I shall not be moved"* (Psalm 16:18). Micah, the prophet, urged *"The breaker is gone up before them: they have broken forth and passed through the gate… Their king is passed on before them, and Jehovah at the head of them"* (Micah 2:13; Exodus 13:21). Indeed, like a warrior, He leads us in any battle, going before us. *"And the angel of God who went before the camp of Israel, removed and went behind them; and the pillar of cloud removed from before them, and stood behind them: it came between the camp of Egypt and the camp of Israel…and the one came not near the other"* (Exodus 14:19-20). Jesus declared, *"If a man loves me He will keep My words: and My Father will love him and We will come unto him, and make our abode with him"* (John 4:23).

We live in a tension between the "now," and the "not yet fully." Jesus declared, *"The kingdom of God has come!"* It is here, now. It is already *"at hand!"* So we are to relax and rejoice. Yet, it is clear that the kingdom has not yet fully come. It is in this "not yet fully" come dimension that we live.

Paul exhorts, *"The Lord is near - at hand!"* It is not clear whether Paul means the imminence of Christ's return or the immediacy of His presence. Both should defy worry. He is coming soon. If He comes today, what do we have to worry about? Until he returns, he is still near, by the presence of the Holy Spirit Right here. He is "at hand" – not far away, present in the pulsating moment though he may be obscured by the shadows. Joy and grace are always signs of his nearness.[2] I recently heard someone say…where!" The coming of Christ is imminent and his presence, immediate. Either way, he is not far from us.

African natives have learned to turn the tables on the lions and stalk them after they have had a successful hunt. With the pride of lions gathered around the fresh kill, a group as small as three warriors approach. The lions are so preoccupied with their meal that they barely notice the warriors. Advancing as one man, in a tight formation, the warriors slowly, silently and fiercely move toward the feasting pride with stone faces. Amazingly, the lions suddenly lift their heads, now aware that they have company for dinner. They fix wary eyes on the warriors. Still approaching slowly, making no sudden moves, now only a few feet away, first one lion and then another, will break for cover, until the entire pride abandons the kill. Finding refuge only a few yards away behind high grass or a thin brush wall, they intently and nervously watch. The warriors say the encounter will not work unless they all exhibit fearless unified confidence that they are superior. Even then, they must

Key Principle

Faith or fear will always travel with us, but never together. Faith causes fear to flee; fear paralyzes faith. The mediating difference is always a sense of God's presence.

quickly carve off an abundant share, leaving sufficient carnage behind for the lions, and do so efficiently, if they are to win an unchallenged battle. The hunters have become the hunted. The tables have been turned. The spoils of the battle have been claimed by another. The roaring lion is now silent.

Faith or fear will always travel with us, but never together. Faith causes fear to flee; fear paralyzes faith. The mediating difference is always a sense of God's presence. When we sense His nearness – fear flees, and faith rises. Even in the valley of the shadow of death, we do not need to fear – *"for Thou art with me!"* Fear is more than a concept. It has a spiritual dimension. David Foster says, "It lives, breathes, mutates, and expands. It attaches to the deepest region of the human heart. And once it has its hooks deeply embedded in its host, it feeds without mercy. Nothing is so sacred that fear won't try to drag it into the gutter and shake the life out of it." Foster continues, "Fear loves to leap into the abyss of irrational thought. It hates truth and beauty. It loves paranoia and innuendo."[4] The Bible declares, *"The wicked flee when no one is chasing them!"* (Proverbs 28:1, TLB) Isaiah says, *"Quietness and stillness shall be your strength"* (Isaiah 30:15). Importing joy and standing in peace while maintaining a clear sense of God's nearness – that is how we are to face life's insecurities! Uncertainties visit us, but uncertainty is not known to God. They may seem imposing, overwhelming to us, but not God.

Difficult times are the breeding ground of invention and discovery. The Civil War, which was not so civil, became an era of innovation. It gave us our first successful submarine, the snorkel, the periscope, aerial reconnaissance, repeating rifles, telescope sights, flares, a steel ship, a highly refined emergency medical corps, hospital ships, ambulance corps, press correspondents, battle photography, the bugle call, wide spread use of anesthetics for the wounded, blackouts and camouflage, and the smoke screen. As the saying goes, necessity is the mother of invention. Tough times spur us to greater levels of creativity.[5]

"If you want to be distressed – look within; if you want to be defeated – look back; if you want to be distracted – look around; and if you want be dismayed – look ahead. But if you want the courage to drive ahead – look up."[6] The power within, by God's grace, is always greater than the task ahead. J. C. Penney built his great network of stores by building people. "Give me a stock clerk with a goal, and I will give you a man who will make history. Give me a man without a goal, and I will give you a stock clerk." The kingdom of God is at hand, and you have been called to be part of it. God has something for you to do.

Pray – As a True Christian

John Dawson has observed, "Everyone prays. Even non-Christians pray. In fact, there is a 'Dial a Prayer' number for atheists now. Call it and it rings, but nobody answers. When Christians pray, they are climbing into the lap of their heavenly Father."[7] They are *inside* the family in a vital relationship with God.

In 1887, surveyors crossed the prairies of the high plains to place the markers along the 49th Parallel, the line that divides the U.S. and Canada. The line ran through the middle of towns and farms, through shops and even houses. Some folks were sleeping in the U.S., and having breakfast in Canada – in their own home. Some thought they were living in the U.S., but discovered that they were on the other side of the line. You must cross a line – a definitive place of repentance and salvation, to pray as a Christian, to enjoy the privileges of access to the heavenly throne room. Everyone can pray. But the Father knows the voices of His own children. Jesus knows the sound of his bride's voice.

We pray from inside, not outside, a relationship with God. Before Jesus, there were only some 40 mentions of God as Father. With the New Covenant, there are at least 260.[8] Paul said it more succinctly, *"Christ in you, the hope of glory"* (Colossians 1:27) – by the Spirit, abiding, indwelling. The Father, by the Spirit, is also present – around us, over us, under us, before us, behind us, and in us.[9]

Psalms and God's Nearness

Psalm 73 stands at the beginning of Book III (Psalms 73–89) in the Psalter,[10] called Josiah's collection, and it sets the tone for entire section. These songs recall Israel's tough times and are loaded with laments. In a difficult season, questions and doubts arise about God's goodness. In Psalm 73, we find unfiltered honesty that reveals a crisis of faith. In it, we move with the psalmist from pervasive uncertainty to a fortified certitude of faith. However, during the journey, he confesses, *"...my feet almost stumbled."*

> *As for me, my feet had almost stumbled; My steps had nearly slipped...when I saw the prosperity of the wicked...the ungodly... are always at ease; They increase in riches. Surely I have cleansed my heart in vain, And washed my hands in innocence.* (73:2-3; 12-13).

The psalm ends on the ground of solid faith, *"I have put my trust in the Lord God!"* Having survived the crisis of faith, he is now emboldened, *"That I may declare all Your works!"* (73:28) Against this struggle, with a world that seems upside down, there is a Hebrew play on the word *good* in the opening and closing verses (73:1, 28). "Truly God is *good to Israel,* to such as are pure in heart. But as for me..." Not wanting to doubt the goodness of God to Israel, the psalmist exempts himself, suggesting some flaw, some impurity of his own heart, that has disqualified him from tasting the goodness of God. But in the end, he claims God's goodness in a personal way, *"But it is good for me to draw near to God; I have put my trust in the*

Lord GOD, That I may declare all Your works." The words serve as a frame through which we view life with its enigmas and disappointments. How do we define *good* in this world? The absolute, unfailing standard is that *"God is good."* And what is *"good for me"* is *"to draw near to God,"* indeed, to *"put my trust in the Lord…"*

The 28 verses of Psalm 73 are in two 14-verse sets. The Hebrew word *'ak,* "surely" is found in the verses in the first section in vv. 1, 13; and in v. 18. Sound faith needs a "surely!" *"Surely,"* the Lord is good. Then he loses his *surely,* and it brings confusion: *"Surely"* (v. 13) – I have cleansed my hands in vain. Faith is for naught. Then clarity is recovered. *"Surely"* – the footing of those who are rich and powerful but faithless is unstable and their security tenuous. The uncertainty is in the twisted reasoning in the Hebrew phrase *we'ani,* translated: *and* or *but.* It is contradictory, back and forth reasoning – *"and…but…"* – an attempt to figure out a world where ungodly people prosper. Here is inner conflict and rattling questions (73:2, 22, 23 and 28). God, if you are good – what about me? Am I an exception to your goodness? He has lost his *surely.* Then he recovers, *"I was so foolish…like a beast before you!"* What was I thinking in that season? I was like a dumb animal. I lost my head for a moment. *"You are continually with me! You hold me by my right hand"* (73:22-23). *"Those who are far from You will perish…But it is good to draw near to You"* (73:28).

Nearness is a *heart* issue. The Hebrew word for heart, *lebab,* is found here six times. The whole struggle is resolved only in the heart, not the head. And the heart, to experience God's nearness, has to be pure (73:2). Two Hebrew expressions are used multiple times (73: 5, 14, 16), *ml,* meaning *burden;* and *ng,* indicating a *plague.* Without a pure heart to inform his thinking, he imagines that his life is plagued. He catastrophizes. Something is dreadfully wrong with him that he is not prospering. Despite God's unseen goodness, he almost abandoned his faith. His eyes had turned to the wealthy and their superficial happiness. The wicked, he concluded, enjoy *shalom* and physical health (73: 4). They have few troubles *('amal)* or woes (v. 5). Honesty demands a closer observation - though they are wealthy, they lack character. Wealth has not made them *better* people, that is, it has not made them *good,* like God. They are proud and violent, with hearts overflowing with conceit. Their language lacks grace, it is oppressive and arrogant.

Fixating on this world and its upside down reward system creates uncertainty. Focusing on God brings clarity. *"I entered the sanctuary of God, then I understood their end!"* (73:17). From the sanctuary, he saw the precarious position of the feet of the wicked – they were on a slippery slope. In the sanctuary, near God, he gained an understanding of the true poverty of the wicked. He realized, he was thinking dumb, *"like a beast"* (v. 22). Only in the sanctuary did he realize that his selfish preoccupation with the *good life* and riches had eclipsed his capacity to see that God had been with him all the time (v. 23). He had momentarily let go; but God had not let go of him. The end of Psalm 73 has an amazingly simple formula. Those who are *"far from you (God) will perish"* (73:27), so, *"It is good for me to draw near to God"* (73:28). The NIV says, *"...it is good to be near God"* (NIV). The NAS, *"The nearness of God is my good".*[11]

Walter Brueggeman says:

The God of the Bible is the strangest thing about the whole Bible. In all the history of religion, there is no other like the God of the Bible...So the people who dwelt with God in the Bible always want to relate to (God) like they relate to all other notions of God. And in every time, even ours today, we are tempted to force God into other categories as though God belongs to a species of similar agents. But God is not like any other. And God's strangeness is in this.

God is with His people. God is for His people. God's goodness is not in the great transcendental power nor in the majestic remoteness nor in the demanding toughness but in the readiness to be with and for people. And being with and for is not a matter of bribery or deception or intimidation. God simply wills it so.[12]

The *Rio Amazonas,* the Amazon, is the second largest river in the world discharging more water than the next seven rivers combined, one-fifth of the world's total river flow. It meanders through the South American rainforest which produces a fifth of the earth's oxygen. The river drives a massive torrent of freshwater into the Atlantic. The surge of water pouring into the ocean is 250 miles long and up to 120 miles wide before it dissipates. Freshwater is lighter, so it overrides the salty sea, diluting the salinity and even altering the ocean color. Ships report fresh water well beyond the sight of land in the open ocean. A hundred miles off-shore, you can dip fresh water. Jesus said, *"Out of your bellies shall flow rivers of living water!"* What could God's certain presence produce through your life?

REVIEW It

1. Lo, I am with you _____.
2. Faith or _____ will travel with you, but never as companions.
3. Though I walk through the valley of the shadow of death, I will fear no evil, for thou art _____.
4. Tough times spur us onward to greater levels of _____.
5. With the New Covenant, the New Testament, there are at least _____ mentions of the fatherhood of God.

TALK About It

1. Share experiences in which a sense of God's presence drove fear away.

2. Talk about the "spiritual dimension" of fear.

3. What is the difference between praying – and prayer from within the new relationship? Ask if members of the group are consciously aware of the difference. Ask if they tend to pray as 'outsiders' or 'insiders.'

4. Talk about the "not yet fully come" kingdom dimension in which we live.

5. Discuss the various "locations" of God, the descriptions of His proximity to us – and what that means.

Endnotes

1. C. Austin Miles, *I Come to the Garden* (March 1912, Public Domain).

2. H. C. G. Moule, *Studies in Philippians* (Grand Rapids, MI: Kregel; 1977), 112.

3. Ibid.

4. Wuest believes the coming of the Lord is in view here. If he is correct, that should evoke joy. It should steady the believer. Most scholars believe what is meant is the immediacy of God's presence. See Kenneth Wuest, *Wuest's Word Studies – Philippians* (Grand Rapids: Eerdmans; 1942), 109.

5. David Foster, *Accept No Mediocre Life: Living Beyond the Labels, Libels, and Limitations* (Hachette Group: New York, 2005), 83.

6. Will Davis, Jr. *Pray Big* (Grand Rapids, MI: Revell, 2007), 30-32.

7. Roy B. Zuck, Compiler, *The Speaker's Quote Book* (Grand Rapids, MI: Kregel Academic, 2009), 145-146.

8. John Dawson, quoted by Pete Krieg and Dave Roberts, 67.

9. Krieg and Roberts, 71.

10. Erich Sauer, *In the Arena of Faith – A Call to the Consecrated Life* (Grand Rapids, MI: Eerdmans; 1966), 80-81.

11. The five subdivisions: Psalms 1-41 – the "Davidic Section" written mostly by David (YHWH occurs 272 times; Elohim 15 times). Psalms 42-72 – "Hezekiah's Collection" (729-696 B.C.; 18 are by David; Elohim appears 200 times, YHWH, 43). Psalms 73-89 – "Josiah's Collection" (638-608 B.C.). Psalms 90-106 – Used in temple worship, only use the name YHWH. Psalms 107-150 – post-exilic collection (after 536 B.C.; nearly all use YHWH; 15 written by David). There are two types of Psalms – the Hallels or "praises" (Psa. 113-118) and the "Songs of Degrees" (Psa. 120-

134).

12. Carl Bosma, "Seeing Clearly in the Sanctuary" (Feb 24, 2011). Posted at: worship.calvin.edu/resources/resource-library/seeing-clearly-in-the-sanctuary-psalm-73 sermon-notes.

13. Walter Bruggeman, *The Bible Makes Sense* (Saint Anthony Messenger Press; 2003), 53.

REVIEW *It Answers*

1. Always
2. Fear
3. With Me
4. Creativity
5. 260

I don't know about tomorrow,
I just live from day to day.
I don't borrow from its sunshine,
For its skies may turn to gray.
I don't worry o'er the future,
For I know what Jesus said,
And today I'll walk beside Him,
For He knows what is ahead.
Ev'ry step is getting brighter,
As the golden stairs I climb;
Ev'ry burden's getting lighter;
Ev'ry cloud is silver lined.
There the sun is always shining,
There no tear will dim the eyes,
At the ending of the rainbow,
Where the mountains touch the sky.
I don't know about tomorrow,
It may bring me poverty;
But the One Who feeds the sparrow,
Is the One Who stands by me.
And the path that be my portion,
May be through the flame or flood,
But His presence goes before me,
And I'm covered with His blood.

Refrain
Many things about tomorrow,
I don't seem to understand;
But I know Who holds tomorrow,
And I know Who holds my hand.[1]

CHAPTER EIGHT
Step Five: Don't Worry About Anything

Be anxious for nothing!

Perspective: Worry is a trigger for fear. Fear is the nemesis of faith, its mortal enemy. Worry tips the first domino and begins a chain reaction – fear, frustration, anger, doubt, faithlessness, despair, depression, hopelessness, revenge, guilt, rage and more. The toxins flow. Our thinking becomes clouded.

Our actions are uncertain. We flee from shadows. We spook over unknown sounds and sights. Paul says, "Don't worry." This is not a prohibition against responsible concern. It is not a lapse in our emotional investment in people or things that matter. Nor is it a prohibition against the bearing of the burden of the Lord or caring deeply. It is a call to trust God in a bold way that allows us to live life in a richer and more positive emotional state. It isn't denial; it is the reality that certain things are beyond our power and "the fix" is with God alone.

"Don't worry" is not a prohibition that stands alone. It is not a solution within itself. It is partnered with positive actions: worship, prayerful pliability, gratitude, passionate petition in which we pour out our pain to God.

Charlotte Elliott was broken. Disabled physically and emotionally by bitterness, she had grown cold and hard. "If God loved me, He would not have treated me this way." There are millions of Charlottes on the earth, all different and alike at the same time. Dr. Cesar Milan visited her on May 9, 1822, hoping to offer some reason for her to escape her chains of cynicism. Charlotte was no easy candidate for conversion. At the table, her mood turned angry and she railed against God in a violent outburst of indignation. All at the table fled before such fury, leaving Dr. Milan and Charlotte alone.

"You are tired of yourself, aren't you?" the pastor stated in matter-of-fact terms. "You are holding on to your hate and anger because you have nothing else in the world to cling to. Consequently, you have become sour, bitter, and resentful." He was peering inside her soul.

Charlotte calmly asked, "What is your cure?" The pastor replied, "The faith you are trying to despise." The conversation deepened. Charlotte softened. "If I wanted to become a Christian, to share the peace and joy you possess, what would I do?" The pastor's simple and forthright answer would prompt a response from Charlotte that is legendary. He told her, "You would give yourself to God just as you are now, with your fightings and fears, hates and loves, pride and shame."

Almost incredulously, obviously expecting a different answer, she replied, with puzzlement, "I would come to God *just as I am?*" She did. On the strength of John 6:37, *"All that the Father gives Me shall come to Me; and him that cometh to Me I will in no wise cast out."* Christ gave her peace, and changed her life. She wrote a poem to capture the spirit of her conversion. Her brother printed it, raising funds for a school for the children of the poor, and the poem became famous across England, *"Sold for the Benefit of St. Margaret's Hall,*

Brighton: Him That Cometh to Me I Will in No Wise Cast Out. "Underneath were the words of Charlotte's conversion poem:

> *Just as I am, without one plea,*
> *But that Thy blood was shed for me,*
> *And that Thou bidd'st me come to Thee,*
> *O Lamb of God, I come. I come!*
> *Just as I am, and waiting not,*
> *To rid my soul of one dark blot,*
> *To Thee whose blood can cleanse each spot,*
> *O Lamb of God, I come! I come.*[2]

Don't Worry – Be Happy

Luther said, "Pray – and let God worry!" Of course, God doesn't worry. And Jesus reminds us that neither do the lilies or the sparrows (Luke 12:13f). God cares for them. If He cares for them, will He not care for us? Why worry? But we do.

Worry's Impact. Jesus advises, *"Therefore do not worry about tomorrow, for tomorrow will worry about itself. Each day has enough trouble of its own"* (Matthew 6:34, NIV). The term translated *worry* is *merimnaó (mer-im-nah'-o)*, meaning, "be not anxious." The Greek word for anxiety comes from *merimna (mer'-im-nah)* meaning cares or concerns and it is related to *merizó (mer-id'-zo)* meaning "to divide." Worry fractures us. It splits our focus. It diverts and diffuses our energy. It injures our capacity to rally our own inner strength. It drains us. We are a house divided against ourselves.

The amygdala is the point in the brain that registers fear and anxiety. It is a neighbor to the hippocampus, the brain's memory system. Strong chemical reactions are triggered when we experience fear and anxiety – and the brain remembers them.[3] Similar experiences are linked together so that the brain records a pattern. When it senses the same scenario or situation, even before the actual experience, just in anticipation of it, the brain and body react. That is commonly called a phobia, an ingrained anxious anticipation with an automated response pattern. Phobias restrict us. They are a psychological-psychosomatic ball and chain. As many as 2.4 million Americans are affected by some kind of panic disorder that overwhelms them at times without a warning.[4] Another 19 million Americans suffer from an anxiety disorder.[5] God wants us free.

A study of 1,700 older men over a 20 year period discovered that men who worried – about social conditions, their health, personal finances, etc. – had a decidedly increased risk of coronary heart disease.[6] It turns out that *peace* really does guard your heart and mind. "Tension causes about 90 percent of all headaches."[7]

Key Principle

Don't worry about anything. Instead, pray about everything. Prayer is to be our first response when trouble comes before joy and peace are disturbed. Worry destabilizes and distracts us. It is deadly to both faith and our witness.

Worry's Cost. While only five percent of people in the culture are categorized as having a general anxiety disorder, the total impact of chronic worriers on the health care system and lost productivity is said to be $22,000 per person per year. Worry is expensive.[8] According to one source, "Stress impairs concentration, causes sleeplessness, and increases the risk for illness, back problems, accidents, and lost time from work…At its most extreme, chronic stress places a burden on the heart and circulation that in some cases may be fatal."[9] Health officials are now saying that chronic stress and its twin, anxiety or worry, may be as much of a fatality risk as smoking or the failure to regularly exercise. As many as 75-90 percent of visits to primary care physicians result from stress-related physical disorders. The body is shouting, like an instrument panel, about some underlying condition.[10]

Worry and Restlessness. We live in a nation of plenty. Food. Toys. Cars. Entertainment. Fine homes. Vacation sites. Golf resorts and dinner theaters. Yet last year, we required 42 million *prescriptions* for sleeping pills, those stronger than the over-the-counter brands.[11] We can't sleep. We can't rest. Anxiety is big business. The rest of the world is glad that water can be found only a few miles away, and we are frustrated that hundreds of channels of entertainment offered through our network provides nothing entertaining. About 40 percent of our time, we worry about things that will never happen. Another 30 percent, we fret about things that cannot be changed, old decisions or mistakes that cannot be reversed. Some 12 percent of our time is spent in attempts to interpret the feelings of others. "Why did he say that? Why did she do that? Why didn't I?" Some 10 percent is spent worrying about our health. Only eight percent of our worrying time is on legitimate issues.[12] Even then, Paul admonishes, "Don't worry."

Modern life threatens rest. In the past 20 years, Americans have added 158 hours a month to work and commuting schedules. "Snooze and lose," is the mantra. Our nightly sleep has shrunk by 20 percent. The lack of rest shows up in an epidemic of daytime drowsiness. The National Sleep Foundation has a "Sleep IQ Test" that 83 percent of Americans flunk. Rest and peace are not topics in which we seem interested.

Worry's Friends. Mentioned earlier, fear and worry are conjoined twins. Fear is faith's greatest enemy. One of the two always travel with us, either fear or faith, but never together. Fear sends faith fleeing; and faith dismisses fear. The mediating factor is the sense of God's presence. *"Yea though I walk through the valley of the shadow of death, I will not fear!"* How is that possible? *"For thou art with me"* (Psalm 23). Worry is a disconnect. It separates us from the nearness of God's presence. The loss of our sense of God's nearness, invites fear.

We tend to see Psalm 23 as metaphorical language, *"Yea, though I walk through the valley of death, I will fear no evil..."* In fact, the passage may not be so allegorical after all. A ten-year study of individuals who could not manage their stress revealed a 40 percent higher death rate than peers.[13] The Mayo Clinic determined that psychological stress was the greatest predictor of a cardiac event – including death by a heart-attack.[14]

The Psalm 23 passage is built to reveal three conditions of life – order, disorder and a new order. The first phase is the valley, green pastures, still waters, plentiful resources, restoration and renewal. The last phase is the high country, the tableland being prepared. There, the believer's cup will be full, their head anointed, goodness and mercy assigned as bodyguards. The middle section is the place of transition and disorder. It is the sheep-drive from the low-county to the high plateau, the transition from winter to summer. It is the place of change, where the dangers have intensified and the transition to the future is uncertain. It is the place where we fall into fear, without a definitive sense of God's presence.

Don't Worry – The Prohibition!

"Be anxious for nothing." Don't worry about anything. The word "nothing" means – not one thing! Allow worry and anxiety no place at all. Paul may have had Psalm 40:17 in mind, *"The Lord thinks on me!"* What a wonderful idea. Worry is deadly to both faith and our witness. It intensifies with attention. It destabilizes and distracts us. Worry, according to James, comes from being too entangled in the *"cares of this world"* (Mark 4:19).

Action One: Don't Worry – Pray. Instead of worrying, we are to pray about everything. Tell God all of your troubles. Prayer is to be our first response when trouble comes. Before joy and peace are disturbed and drained away by some mounting pressure, pray. Joy may chase away worry and change our affect, but it doesn't solve the problem. The difficulty may still be glaring at us. Only God can remove the actual obstacle. Only heaven can address the real trouble.

Spurgeon urged,

> There is no need for us to go beating about the bush, and not telling the Lord distinctly what it is that we crave at His hands. Nor will it be seemly for us to make any attempt to use fine language: but let us ask God in the simplest and most direct manner for just the things we want.[15]

Action Two: Don't Let Automated Responses Reign. Sin did more than separate us from God. Because of sin in the human family, we are born and shaped in iniquity, with predispositions that are now native, and yet non-productive and self-destructive. *Frustration*, psychologists tell us, is our attempt to control the uncontrollable. *Fear* is our negative and often debilitating response to something we dread, unknown or unseen. *Hurt* is our reaction to pain, physical or emotional. All three of these – *frustration, fear and hurt* – trigger anger and put us into an agitated state. In every case, the physiological response mechanisms are automated. We react, often before we think. These impulse responses are wired into our damaged psyches. Only a person who disciplines himself to become acutely self-aware will recognize the inner signals in such moments. Fight or flight is a native response and that flesh-pattern is memorized in our brain. We react quickly and do so without a thorough rational process. Frustration multiplies. Fear motivates us. Hurt sends us recoiling into some corner or aggressively defending ourselves against further pain.

Action Three: Don't React, Act. Paul is revealing the secret to short-circuit these natural reactive flesh-patterns. First, you and I are not to *react*, but to *act*. We are encouraged to play offense before the problem comes. We should never stop rejoicing. And when a challenge to our joy surfaces, it is imperative that we defy flesh-based response patterns and verbalize joy. At such a time, we need to hear ourselves rejoicing. In that way, we diffuse the world's negative energy. Our inner gyroscope steadies us.

We not only refuse to worry – but simultaneously, we worshipfully pray and offer our supplication with thanksgiving. We cry out to God asking for his intervention – "we request" heaven's aid. This requires an inner re-training. Saved, we still react as we did before we became Christians. We panic rather than praise. We worry rather than worship. We remain under the world's load, rather than focusing on how well we are carrying the weighty glory of God. We have not yet fully embraced the disciplines of a Biblically ordered life.

Rejoice, and keep on rejoicing! Make happy sounds. Do so on the basis of Christ's finished work, not in keeping with your own emotional state. Keep your nose up. Stay steady. Be gentle and gracious. Don't allow yourself to adopt an attitude that will cause you to crash. Pray. Be thankful. Those are not the typical ways we react to life's problems.

Action Four: Don't Lie To God. Luther's number one rule for prayer was "Don't lie to God!" In fact,

> Raw honesty in prayer is like a volatile liquid, powerful if used right, destructive if dropped or shaken. Trapped in our belief that we can never say what is really on our heart, we can be polite with God and submerge our real emotions and real issues.[16]
>
> Good praying is bare-knuckle praying. It is real, sometimes tearful, always authentic and genuine. We talk to God in every possible manner: desperately, impatiently, fearfully, needfully, thankfully, joyfully, in tears, at a loss for words, and sometimes even angrily. There is no time, no mood, that can keep me apart from Him. Not anymore.[17]

Action Five: Pray Through. The old-timers talked about praying until you *"prayed through."* Praying through is passionate and determined praying that persists until there is an answer. It wrestles with a concern, prayerfully approaching it in various ways, sizing it up, and dressing it down. It *"prays through"* the issues created by the problem in a systematic way. It searches by the Spirit and in the Word for answers. It calls out to God for wisdom. It dares to triumph in the face of difficulty. It rises from prayer with a deep assurance, "God is going to answer my prayer. I have what I have asked for." At other times, *"praying through"* is praying until you have delivered your soul. You may not have the assurance God is going to grant your petition, but you know He has heard your prayer. In that you rest. You have peace. You have a song. You have, by grace, poise under pressure.

Any trouble is a reason to pray! We are to continue *"instant in prayer"* (Romans 12:12). It should not be a strange thing for a Christian, especially in a group of believers, to open a conversation with God – spontaneously, almost casually, naturally – in public. At a restaurant table. In a park around a campfire. In the middle of an accident scene. In a hospital corridor. Instant prayer – everywhere, anytime. Paul's habit was to pray – then and there, when the trouble first appeared and to offer thanks to God for the solution before it could be seen in the natural. Daniel labored in prayer for 21 days, and the angel who broke through reported, *"...from the first day that you set your heart to understand, and to humble yourself before God, your words were heard"* (Daniel 10:12-13).

Action Six: Don't Hesitate. George Cecil declared, "On the Plains of Hesitation, bleach the bones of countless millions who, at the dawn of victory, sat down to wait, and waiting – died!"[18] Hesitation is a form of doubt. It is a lapse in faith. It opens the door that lets in worry and fear and they paralyze. But the prohibition, "Don't worry!" is not enough. It is like telling a child, "Go sit in that corner and don't think about the ice cream everyone else is having". How can he not think about ice cream? So, Paul loads us up with positive action options, not merely a prohibition – pray, tell God the problem, give thanks in the face of the need. Hesitation is fear's opportunity. It caused Peter to pause on the water and sink. It caused Gideon's indecision. It trapped Israel in the wilderness for 40 years. "Why halt ye between two opinions," Elijah charged. The indecision of hesitation is deadly.

Lefty Gomez was a great legendary pitcher for the New York Yankees and a Hall of Famer. But, he was a lousy hitter, garnering only a few hits over the course of the entire season. He was a sure out for any opposing team. Once, he quite accidentally connected with the ball and got a solid double. The second baseman asked him to step off the bag so he could straighten it up. Gomez did and was promptly tagged out. He returned dejectedly to the dugout, his moment of triumph turned sour, Joe McCarthy, the manager asked Lefty, "What happened out there?" Gomez shook his head innocently and said, "How should I know...I've never been out there before."

Whatever new or strange place in which you find yourself, God can give grace. When Luther was on trial, he would not relent or recant. The Cardinal grew impatient with him. Wanting to decisively end what he considered a minor and regional problem from becoming something international, he thundered at Luther with the line that was suggested to Rehoboam by his young advisors (I Kings 12:10), "The Pope's little finger is stronger than all of Germany. Do you expect your princes to take up arms to defend you – a wretched worm like you? I tell you, No! And where will you be then?" Rehoboam had listened to such arrogant counsel, and it split the kingdom. Now, it would divide Europe. Without hesitation, Luther replied, "Then, as now, I shall be in the hands of God." No one at that meeting could have guessed the outcome of Luther's resolution – the Protestant Reformation.

REVIEW It

1. Luther said, "_____ and let God worry!"
2. _____% of our time is spent worrying about what never happens.
3. _____ is to be the first response when we are tempted to worry.
4. Be anxious for _____.
5. The old timers used the term praying until you have prayed _____.

TALK About It

1. Ask your group if they understand the concept of 'praying through?' Practice it, as a group.
2. Discuss the concept of 'worry' as a divided mind.
3. What has worry cost you?
4. When has "hesitation" cost you a victory?
5. Talk about the Old Testament concept of "turning" as a part of the inner renewal at work in the life of a new convert.

Endnotes

1. Ira F. Stanphill, "I Don't Know About Tomorrow" (Singspiration, A Division of Zondervan, 1953; Now: Brentwood Benson Music).
2. Morgan, *More Real Stories,* 41-42.
3. Don Colbert, *Deadly Emotions: Understanding the Mind-Body-Spirit Connection That Can Heal or Destroy You* (Nashville: Thomas Nelson; 2003), 98.
4. Ibid, 106.
5. Ibid, 108.
6. L. D. Kubzansky, I. Kawachi, A. Spirio III, Etc, "Is Worrying Bad for Your Heart? A Prospective Study of Worry and Coronary Heart Disease in the Normative Aging Study," (Circulation, 94; 1997), 818-824.
7. Colbert, 110.
8. Staff Writers: Reuters, "Neurotic People Can Each Cost Society

$22,000 a Year" (NYDailyNews.com; Wednesday, October 06, 2010). See: articles.nydailynews.com/2010-10-06/entertainment/27077365_1_mental-illness-neuroticism-mental-health.

9. "Anxiety In-depth Report" (New York Times, On-line). See – health.nytimes.com/health/guides/symptoms/stress-and-anxiety/print.html.

10. P. Rosch, "Job Stress: America's Leading Adult Health Problem," (USA Today, May 1991), 42-44.

11. "Insomnia or Sleep Loss? What are the Signs? How To Power Nap for Insomnia!" www.healthdiscoveries.net/insomnia.html.

12. Archibald Hart, *The Anxiety Cure* (Nashville, TN: Thomas Nelson Inc, 2001). Original source: Dr. J. Cronin.

13. H. J. Eysenck, "Personality, Stress, and Anger: Prediction and Prophylaxis," (British Journal of Medical Psychology, 1988), 57-75; 61.

14. T. G. Allison, D. E. Williams, T. D. Miller, etc., "Medical and Economic Costs of Psychologic Distress in Patients with Coronary Artery Disease," (Mayo Clinic Proceedings, 70; 1995), 734-742.

15. Author Unknown, *The Kneeling Christian* (Kessinger Publishing, 2004), 79.

16. Greig and Roberts, *Red Moon Rising – How 24-7 Prayer is Awakening a Generation* (Eastbourne, England: Relevant Books, Kingsway Publications; 2003), 163-164.

17. Phyllis Hobe, *The GuidePosts Handbook of Prayer* (New York: Smith Mark Publishers, a Division of US Media Holdings, Inc.; 1982), 7.

18. Suzy Platt, *Respectfully Quoted: A Dictionary of Quotations*, (Barnes and Noble Books, 1989, 1993), 342. . Accessed – June 6, 2011. See also: Susan A. Nielsen, "Wake Up To The Reality Of Sleep Deprivation" (Newhouse News Service: Seattle Times; Thursday, June 22, 2006).

REVIEW It Answers

1. Pray
2. 40
3. Prayer
4. Nothing
5. Through

When we walk with the Lord
in the light of His word,
what a glory He sheds on our way!
While we do His good will,
He abides with us still,
and with all who will trust and obey.

Refrain: Trust and obey, for there's no other way
to be happy in Jesus, but to trust and obey.

Not a burden we bear,
not a sorrow we share,
but our toil He doth richly repay;
not a grief or a loss,
not a frown or a cross,
but is blest if we trust and obey.

But we never can prove
the delights of His love
until all on the altar we lay;
for the favor He shows,
for the joy He bestows,
are for them who will trust and obey.

Then in fellowship sweet
we will sit at His feet,
or we'll walk by His side in the way;
what He says we will do,
where He sends we will go;
never fear, only trust and obey.[1]

CHAPTER NINE
Steps Six and Seven: Worship and Be Flexible

In everything, by prayer and supplication…

Perspective: The key to new life in Christ is not bound up in what we don't do! Christianity is not about prohibition. It demands positive action. Be worshipful. Change your focus. Be flexible. Be adaptable. Our watching friends see the impact of such altered behavior. They see the new way we talk and walk.

What difference does it make, when one man, even a boy or girl, makes peace with God? When an individual, in view of the cross, the mercy of God, decides to trade their life for the life in Christ – how significant is such a moment? In heaven, we are told, there is a celebration (Luke 15:7). On earth, we barely notice.

On a nasty January Sunday in 1850 with blizzard conditions, almost no one showed up at church that morning, not even the preacher. A handful of hardy and faithful worshippers waited for a season, and then a humble old fellow, a common laborer, rose to offer a few words of encouragement. It was a miserable attempt at preaching, but no one expected much of anything to happen that day anyway. However, something did happen, something that would influence the world. A fifteen year-old boy, unable to reach his own church, sought refuge in the little Primitive Methodist building, and in the service was moved to make Christ his Savior and Lord. The young lad was not only saved, he soon felt a call to ministry. Before the age of 20, he had preached 600 times. Before the end of his life, he was the most popular preacher in London, preaching regularly to crowds of five-to-six thousand. His sermons were printed in 20 languages and each copy sold some 25,000. His collection of sermons, 53 volumes, is the largest set of books by a single author in the history of Christianity. The boy saved on that wintry day was Charles Spurgeon.[2]

STEP SIX: Worship

Do Worshipful Praying. First, we are to "pray" – here is a *worship* word always used of approaching God. It conveys the meaning of reverence,[3] of turning our face toward God and seeking Him. Don't fixate on the problem. Turn your face away from it and toward God. This is not denial. Rather, it is a reorientation toward the solution so as to not be paralyzed by the problem. Isaiah urged Israel to be courageous and leave Babylon to return to Israel. *"The time of your warfare is over,"* he decreed. *"Every valley shall be exalted, every mountain shall be made low. The crooked places will be made straight and the rough places smooth."* Going home would not be easy, but the prophet suggested that God would make the route itself easier.

Israel resisted. They lacked the faith to believe they could return home, despite the urging of the prophet. *"All flesh is grass and the goodliness thereof as the flower of the field. The grass withers and the flower fades"* (Isaiah 40:6, 8). It was true. Human effort would not be enough. Like the hot summer sun that quickly withered the tender grass and stripped the spring flowers of beauty, their strength would fade in the face of the obstacles they would encounter. *"But,"* the prophet countered, *"The word of the Lord will endure forever!"* They were not to start the journey home to restoration on the strength of human zeal or a mere prophet's word, but on the strength of God's Word. When they further despaired, the prophet urged, *"Get thee up on a high mountain and behold your God."* What follows is one of most powerful descriptions of God anywhere in Scripture. If they could climb the mountain, get above the world's woes, and get a clear view of God, faith would rise. Who hasn't clung to the last few lines of Isaiah 40? *"They that wait upon the Lord shall renew their strength, they shall mount up like the wings of the eagle, they shall run and not be weary, they shall walk and not faint."* The secret of the eagle's flight is that he reads the wind currents and rides the thermal draft. He "mounts up" on the invisible air, soaring effortlessly higher and higher. So we must learn to ride the wind of the Spirit. Our victory is not won by spending ourselves, but by being empowered by the Holy Spirit.

Key Principle

Never look first for an *answer* from God, look first to the God who answers. You will never pray beyond your revelation and understanding of God.

See the God Who Answers. Never look first for an *answer* from God, look first to God who answers. Seek Him. When Jesus taught on prayer, He instructed us to "ask, seek and knock." Asking involves petitions for *things*. Seeking involves going after *God Himself*. Good praying may begin with needs, but better praying takes place when we lay the need aside and realize that an answer is not as important to us as God Himself. Seek Him. Knocking opens a doorway to a solution or perhaps a whole new dimension – a new way of viewing the problem or even life itself. Perhaps, to a new world of provision. And that is the other side of seeking - a focus on God!

You will never pray beyond your revelation and understanding of God. If you know God only as a redeemer, that is where you will pray. If you have learned that He is also a healer, you will have confidence to pray for healing. The more you focus, not merely on answers, but on God Himself, on knowing Him, the deeper your prayer life will grow.

Stay Focused. Our culture teaches the value of an *open* mind. The Bible actually teaches quite the opposite. We are to *"gird up the loins of our mind."* What an odd expression. It seems a bit explicit, and it is. Paul is concerned that the unguarded mind will give birth to godless notions. A wandering mind, a major ailment in prayer, is like an open garden in which anyone can sow seed. A radically open mind, one with no filters, no truth lens or standard, is an opportunity for the Evil One. If you can't discipline your thoughts, you can't pray. The 'open gates' allow thoughts to come and go in an indiscriminate way creating a mental mine field, ripe for an explosion.

STEP SEVEN: Stay Flexible

Supplication, the second word in our passage, is from *supple* which means to *bend.* It is sometimes translated *beseech.* It involves intensity and earnestness beyond serious asking. We have two choices – the world and its problems can bend and shape us; or we can bend before God in prayer and let him shape our problems and us. Talk to God. Detail the problem. Passionately tell God your fears. Any pressure should move us to prayer. Supplication reminds us that in the face of problems, we are not to be rigid. Firm and grounded in God's word and promises? Yes! Yet still pliable and open for God to work in mysterious ways to accomplish his will.

Buried – Yet Still Walking Around

Christians, true Christians, are dead – to sin and self! Each has stood by faith at the cross and identified with Christ. They have witnessed what sin did to Christ at the cross, and repented of sinful attitudes and actions. The wages of sin brought eternal death. However, God at the cross did what only God could do! (1 Peter 2:24-25) He split the impact of death that came by sin. Jesus died there physically, and the power of sin died there as well (1 Cor. 15:56; Rom. 6). But death could not claim either his spirit or his soul. He was without sin. In the final moments of his life, he embraced our sins. He took the deadly load of sin from us and *"became sin who knew no sin, that we might be made in the righteousness of God"* (2 Cor. 5:21). Jesus tasted death – in his body, that you and I might be spared eternal death. By the mercy of God, we are alive – after facing judgment before a Holy God at Calvary, through Christ. He descended into the grave, into the jaws of death, carrying our sin with him. We were raised to new life, in his resurrection. While we are alive – we are counted as dead.

There is one primary reason we are left on the earth after our conversion, after we have died to sin! Baptized in a watery grave, buried (Colossians 2:12), we acknowledge symbolically that the wages of sin are death (Romans 3:23), and that sin itself is deadly. In that moment, we bury the old way of living. We count ourselves as dead, as if the disease of sin had won its battle over our life and claimed us. And then we emerge from the water, as if 'born again,' to begin a second life.

In baptism, we participate in our own funeral service. The old is gone, the new is raised. The life dedicated to self is no more; a life dedicated to God is emerging. This is the exchanged life. We are dead to the world, dead to sin and self, but alive to God. We have been *"crucified with Christ! Nevertheless, we live, and yet it is not we that live, but Christ in us, the hope of glory"* (Colossians 1:27). To that end, kneeling keeps you in good standing.

Our Unfinished Business

We have an unfinished task – the Great Commission. We cannot complete that calling unless we live such lives before a watching world that they offer compelling evidence of the reality of Christ, the truth about his resurrection, his enthronement, his kingdom in exile, his soon and certain return. Here is the converging theme – my life is a witness. The purpose of that witness is evangelism. We are a light in the midst of darkness (1 Peter 2:9). Salt in the midst of decay (Matthew 5:13-16). There is an enemy to our faith who has come to steal, kill and destroy (John 10:10). He is the force behind the invisible guerilla movement in the earth now, the counter-kingdom to Christ and the Church, as well as the push toward godless globalism. He now operates from the middle heaven with the intent to establish his dark kingdom on the earth, to promote and enforce allegiance to his own universal faith. He will anoint his own prophetic and political leaders – the false prophet and the anti-Christ, though the world will not identify them as such. You and I, as believers, are obstacles to his purposes.

God in heaven is depending on us to complete the Great Commission, to disciple the nations with true truth and to do so in the spirit of the Great Commandment – love. There is no backup plan. For 2,000 years, we have left the task unfinished. Lucifer is deluded, but nevertheless convinced, that we will not finish the task. Indeed, he seems convinced that he can induce the world to embrace him through his surrogate, the False Prophet, a Messianic figure. Then crown his representative, though he will be thoroughly anti-Christian, as this world's king, moving the earth to reject Christ again, with his bride, the Church, tasting the bitter cross of martyrdom and persecution.

Increasingly, Christianity is viewed as too narrow, too morally confining, too exclusive and inflexible, as lacking unqualified personal affirmation and the right to self-definition. The demand for repentance and self-negation, for submission and redirection are viewed as negative, self-censuring, too rigid and absolute to be self-styled. To such philosophical shifts, Lucifer is irresponsibly committed.

Every person has a network of a dozen or so close friends – family, neighbors, work associates, sports or shopping buddies, confidents, business associates. Some of them are saved, some are not. In all, we have some 100 acquaintances. These are people with whom we occasionally interact – the druggist, the cable-guy, a smiling grocer, a favorite waiter – and dozens more. In some cases, we may not even know their names. Yet, we touch their lives. God uses our life as a stage to reveal Himself to these people. He does not exempt us from trouble, but delivers us from and through it – for His glory, with the eyes of fellow travelers watching us. He does not exempt us from temptation or seemingly delicious offers from the Evil One. Our circle of friends may know about the godless opportunity. They may even be in on the diabolical deal. Our refusal to bow is a testimony. Especially if it involves saying, 'No!' to the idol of compromise. Especially if we are promised riches or power in exchange for some moral concession which we decline. Especially if the offer involves our ingratiation or invitation into some exclusive circle of worldly influencers and we refuse the offer.

Life brings trouble. Not every problem is a direct demonic attack, but some problems are designed in hell. When Haman attempted to trick the King and thereby execute Mordecai and Esther, the Evil One drove the process. Evil men laid a trap for Daniel to be caught praying to an unauthorized deity and for that reason executed, certainly the hand of the Evil One was in the mix. When the heart of Judas was inspired by Satan to turn against Jesus, the tide of troubles surrounding the cross were driven by evil energy. And yet, even that action was within the sovereign surveillance of God. The Father used that moment to bring glory to Himself and through the cross to save us. So with us, life brings us trouble, but in the sovereign design of God, even trouble is turned to our advantage and to God's glory.

Our Wily Adversary

Satan is guilty of shedding the blood of Jesus. He is incorrigible and beyond redemption.[4] God, knowing his diabolical character, watches over us. Satan most often works in the midst of trouble. He neither has to design it or drive it, only exploit it. The world and the flesh bring us trouble. And when it comes, usually in clusters, Lucifer and his aides delight in whispering to us in the middle of life's storms. They induce us to react. They falsely report that the storms will increase and destroy us. They shout out doubt and despair. They distort Biblical promises. They war against our clear thinking in moments of trouble.

Two means are used by Lucifer to cause us to bolt and run, to collapse on the stage of life, to fail to be a witness before our family and friends – the psychological pressure of the trial and the temptation to do wrong. The Bible calls this *deception*. With it, forms of confusion come – a smoke and mirror delusion. And Satan also uses *accusation,* a form of condemnation. These are despairing and discouraging accusations about God or us and about the nature of our relationship with God. All lies. Nothing life delivers can overcome or overwhelm us. Nothing! The problem is always in flawed thinking and our attempt at self-sufficiency, prayerlessness. Even if we are mediocre Christians living reasonably moral lives – we go to church, we say a blessing over our food even at a public restaurant, we don't use foul language and we are not coarse in our personal actions. Even if we are not blazing lights - only lukewarm witnesses. Even that moderate level of light penetrating the darkness is unreasonable to

Lucifer. God's presence in us is an obstacle to Lucifer's purposes. Our worship, evangelizing and disciple making is at cross-purposes with his dark kingdom.

For that reason alone, we can expect uncanny life episodes designed to deter us. Not every flat tire is to be interpreted as "spiritual warfare." Still, there are times when we step into life situations that resemble the chaos of an intersection when traffic lights malfunction. Times, when the rain is so heavy that visibility is nearly impossible and accidents are virtually assured. Such dangerous moments are occasions for the Evil One. Even if he is not behind their design, he is often at work in the midst of such confusion to create havoc. Have you noticed that such events come in bunches? And often, they come on the eve of the launch of some

Key Principle

We have two choices – the world and its problems can bend and shape us; or we can bend before God in prayer and let him shape our problems and us.

godly mission? Or they come in the middle of some critical assignment? At such times, we can hardly afford to be delayed.

There are pressures from the outside that are real. And there are whispers from the edges of the darkness to allure us to leave the righteous path and wander into the shadowy wastelands of sin. Whether the pressure is external – a test; or internal – a temptation, a solicitation to evil, the end result is the same. If we succumb, we are temporarily or permanently "out of service" as an effective witness. Even if our relationship with God is renewed, and fervently so, after the wreck or the momentary defection from the righteous path, for some season our witness is hindered, perhaps even damaged. Prayer is no instant cure. No magic baton. In prayer, you deal with entrenched foes, set and determined wills. Duewel says, "You may have to environ them for days with prayer before they understand or become willing to obey God. Prayer answers often require complex coordinating and timing of events and lives by God."[5] Duewel argues, "You cannot store up grace, but you can store up prayer. Mounting flood waters can sweep away any obstruction and burst any dam. In the same way, the accumulated power of prevailing prayer can move immovable obstacles." We must pray without ceasing. Duewel says this is not so much an action, as it is an attitude. [6]

Our Walk and Its Message

From Genesis onward, the Scripture emphasizes the *walk* of believers. Biblical faith is never a mere philosophy, but a way of life. It may be easier to *preach ten* sermons than it is to *live one*, but what God seems to value is the one lived. Genesis 17:1 exhorts – *"walk before God and be blameless."* Enoch, we are told, *"walked with God"* and God took him (Genesis 5:22, 24). In Exodus, the children of Israel followed the cloud (Exodus 40:36; Numbers 9:17-18). In Leviticus, we are urged to walk in His statutes (Leviticus 26:3). In Deuteronomy, we are commanded to walk in all His ways (10:12). Psalm 84:11 advises us to walk uprightly.

Similar admonitions are found throughout the Old Testament. In the New Testament, we meet them again. Romans 6:4 declares, *"Walk in newness of life,"* and 8:1, *"Walk in the Spirit."* 2 Corinthians commands, *"Walk by faith and not by sight."* And in Ephesians, we meet an abundance of walk admonitions – *"walk worthy"* of the calling on your life (4:1); walk *righteously* (4:17f); walk in *love* (5:2); walk in *light* (5:8); walk *circumspectly,* with balance (5:15). Of course, our walk and our talk go together. Someone has succinctly said, "Put both feet in your mouth at the same time, and you won't have a leg to stand on."

It was said of Marie Antoinette that "when she walked, she

strode like a man. Her swift, purposeful gait was her trademark. It was said that she could never successfully disguise her identity at masked balls, for no matter how she dressed, she still walked like the Empress."[7] Our Christ-like walk is to tell on us as well. So pervasive should the change be in us, that we cannot mask our identity - we are the followers of Jesus Christ.

REVIEW It

1. The God of peace gives the gift of _____.
2. We are left on the earth to finish the Great _____.
3. God uses our lives as a platform or stage to _____ Himself.
4. The two means by which Lucifer works are _____ and _____.
5. We are to be _____ in the midst of decay; and _____ in the darkness.

TALK About It

1. How is God glorified by our lives in the midst of trouble?
2. Discuss the idea: "Life is a stage. We are the actors and the world is watching."
3. Make a list of people around you whom you would like to have a positive influence on for Christ.
4. Are you a 'ten,' leading the class, or a 'one,' with too many around you not even knowing that you are a Christ-follower? Rate the quality of your witness before your friends and neighbors.
5. Talk about "baptism" as the death of self and our lives as "living sacrifices" offered to God.

Endnotes

1. John H. Sammis, *Trust and Obey* (Copyright: Public Domain, 1887).
2. Morgan, *More Stories,* 106-107.
3. Stuart Briscoe. *Bound for Joy* (Glendale, CA: Gospel Light; 1975), 141.
4. Wesley Duewel, *Touch the World Through Prayer* (Zondervan, 1986), 120.
5. Ibid, 199.
6. Ibid.
7. Morgan, *More Stories,* 99-100.

REVIEW It Answers

1. Peace
2. Commission
3. Reveal
4. Deception and Accusation
5. Salt and Light

I trust in God wherever I may be,
Upon the land or on the rolling sea,
For, come what may, from day to day,
My heav'nly Father watches over me.
He makes the rose an object of His care,
He guides the eagle thru the pathless air,
And surely He remembers me,
My heav'nly Father watches over me.
I trust in God, for in the the lion's den,
On battlefield, or in the prison pen,
Thru praise or blame, thru flood or flame,
My heav'nly Father watches over me.
The valley may be dark, the shadows deep
But O, The Shepherd guards His lonely sheep;
And thru the gloom, He'll lead me home
My heav'nly Father watches over me.

Chorus
I trust in God, I know He cares for me,
On mountain bleak or on the stormy sea;
Tho' billows roll, He keeps my soul,
My heavn'ly Father watches over me.[1]

CHAPTER TEN
Step Eight: Wrap Your Requests in Thanksgiving

In everything...with thanksgiving,
let your requests be known to God.

Perspective: In the face of the need and want, we offer thanks. 'In' everything, though not 'for' everything, we give thanks. In the midst of the storm, we push back torment with thanksgiving. It is not enough to resist the devil, we must also submit to God.

It is not enough to not do unrighteousness, we must act in righteous ways (Romans 6). We meet pain with praise. We dance in the face of depression, breaking the spirit of heaviness, wearing the garment of praise. This is defiant faith. This is a quest for another reality. It is a refusal to be pushed and pulled by the world. It is David declaring, when hope is low, "Yet, I will praise him..." (Psalm 42:5). It is Abraham, counting the stars, at the age of 99. It is John, seeing the resurrected Christ on Patmos with the keys of death and hell.

The majority of the world lives without the hope offered by Christ. The open door to God's throne is a unique post-resurrection-ascension-enthronement Christian notion and unique privilege. That we can pray, pour out our souls to a God who cares, is an incredible privilege. That we get answers from God is beyond incredible. Sadly, prayer is now seen as passé. It is the most under-utilized privilege afforded believers. The average American Christian prays only four minutes a day. God leaves his door open and invites us to visit and bring our troubles, doing so with gratitude in view of his previous grants. When heaven answers our prayer, we should not be silent about such a benevolent God.

Calling God

In the movie *Bruce Almighty,* a seven-digit number that flashed on Jim Carrey's display was purportedly God calling. Usually, carefully chosen non-functioning numbers are used in movies. In that movie, the number displayed was a functioning number, at least, when paired with some area codes. A phenomenon followed the airing of the movie across the nation. People added an area code and started calling the number – presumably calling "God!" Those who received the calls "to God" quickly caught on. Many played along. Some found desperate callers on the other end of the line.

A call to a Colorado Network was from a woman behind bars. Only reaching an answering machine did not deter her from leaving a poignant message, "I'm in jail right now. Like I said to you last night, 'I love you.'" She assured God she was going to change the way she was living and requested His help to return to her family. One person called the number and admitted that they knew this wasn't the number for God, but wondered if there was another! One medical supervisor, whose seven-digit number matched that shown on the screen was getting as many as 40-50 calls a day shortly after the movie aired. People want to talk to God.[2]

God's Invitation – "Call Me!"

Jeremiah, the weeping prophet who witnessed the demise of Judah, the destruction of the Temple, and the exile of his Jewish brothers, never lost faith in the power of prayer. *"Call to Me and I will answer you and tell you great and unsearchable things you do not know"* (Jeremiah 33:3, NIV). An unknown poet wrote, "When God inclines the heart to pray, He hath an ear to hear; To Him there's music in a groan, and beauty in a tear."[3] The desire to pray itself is evidence of God's work in the heart. It is by grace that we pray.

Key Principle

Just the privilege of prayer is worthy of joy and gratefulness. We rejoice, confident that there is someone on the other end of the line. To withhold our gratitude unless God performs to our expectations indicates the degree to which pride controls our lives.

A Gallup poll some years ago revealed surprising facts about prayer. Some 88 percent of Americans pray to God in one way or another, but only 42 percent dared ask God for material or tangible things – a surprisingly low number. And only 15 percent said they regularly experienced answers to specific requests.[4] God says, "Call me sometime!"

God's Compassionate Nature

"In your love you kept me from the pit of destruction" Isaiah declared (Isaiah 38:17). The psalmist recalled, *"O LORD, You brought me up from the grave. You called me back to life from among those who had gone into the pit"* (Psalm 30:3, GWT). We rejoice first that there is a God. Then we are grateful He hears us when we pray, and He cares about us as a loving Father. Prayer is about the relationship, before it is about the benefits.

Just the privilege of prayer is worthy of joy and gratefulness. We rejoice, confident that there is someone on the other end of the line. To withhold our gratitude unless God performs to our expectations indicates the degree to which pride controls our lives. He is God, we are the servants. Prayer is no magic lantern to be rubbed and God is no genie who is there to blindly grant our wishes. That is a pagan idea of prayer! The idea of a compassionate God who hears us weeping in the night and cares is matchless among the religions of the world. And it is distinctively a Christian-Jewish notion.

God's Promises

Pray about everything. God is both a promising God and a giving God. If something is big enough to worry about, it is big enough for prayer. Apart from the Psalms, there are 650 prayers recorded in Scripture with 450 answers. God answers prayer. He fulfills His promises. He keeps His covenant. And He uses prayer as a part of that process.[5] There are 7,959 promises in the Bible. If we use one promise each day it will take us 22 years to use each of the promises once.[6] Caleb lived 40 years on one promise. How many years can we live on 7,959 promises? Armin Gesswein said:

> Promises predict the answers to prayer. They are the molds into which we pour our prayers. They foretell what to expect. They shape our praying. They motivate, direct and determine our supplication…This makes Christian praying different! How? In a very real sense we pray from the answer…with the answer in mind…from the answer to it. This is the way of The Lord, the way of faith. He promises – we believe. We act on His Word. In this way answered prayer not only satisfies us; it delights the Heart of God by fulfilling His Own Word. And this is a most important thing with God.[7]

When you are praying for a certain thing, search the Scripture, and see what God has promised. Then pray the Scripture. Stand on the promise. Jeremiah (33:19-27) declared that God's promises to David were as dependable as the rising and setting sun.

If you can break My covenant with the day and My covenant with the night, so that day and night no longer come at their appointed time then My covenant with David My servant can be broken.

The Scripture makes it clear, *"God is not a man that He should lie nor a son of man that He should change His mind. Does He speak and then not act? Does He promise and not fulfill?"* (Numbers 23:19).

D. L. Moody once said, "Tarry at a promise and God will meet you there." Armin Gesswein, early in his ministry, discovered a principle that changed his ministry. He was a 24-year-old church planter on Long Island. What he found was called the "prayer meeting truth" of Acts. The prayer meeting he started was the first one he ever attended. An elderly Methodist man came into the meeting one night, Ambrose Whaley.

Gesswein said, "When he prayed I detected something new. I had never heard praying like that." The prayers and the answers were not far apart. Gesswein examined his lack, knowing his heart was fervent, but something was missing. The old Methodist was praying with a confidence the young church planter lacked.

The Holy Spirit was right here, in action, giving him assurance of the answer even while he was praying! When I prayed, God was 'way out there' listening in the distance somewhere. The answer, too, was in the distance, totally unreachable.

Eager to learn, Armin went to see "Uncle Am" as he was called, a retired blacksmith and lay preacher. "Uncle Am, I would love to pray with you." The old man rose immediately. He led the young preacher across a driveway, into a barn, and up a ladder into a haystack! There, amidst the hay, were two Bibles, one laying open. He had never seen the likes, "What is this?" Am gave no explanation, he simply invited Armin to pray.

"I poured out my heart, needs, burdens, wishes, aspirations, ambitions to God." And then, Am prayed. Armin said, "There was 'that difference' again." Both men were on their knees in the hay, "Uncle Am, what is it? You have some kind of secret in praying. Would you mind sharing it with me?" Armin recalls, "I was 24. He was 73. With the look of an eagle in his eye, he urged, 'Young man, learn to plead the promises of God!'" That insight changed Armin forever. He would become legendary in his prayer walk. And he would confess, "My praying has never been the same since. That word completely changed my understanding of prayer. It really revolutionized it! I 'saw it' as soon as he said it." Before,

> When I prayed there was fervency and ambition...but I lacked faith. 'Prayer is the key to heaven, but faith unlocks the door.' There must be faith. Where does that come from? From hearing...the Word of God. Uncle Am would plead Scripture after Scripture, reminding God of promise after promise, pleading these like a lawyer does his case, the Holy Spirit pouring in His assurance of being heard. This man knew the promises 'by the bushel.' He did not seem to need those Bibles in that hay! I soon learned that he was a mighty intercessor. He prayed 'clear through.' He prayed using the Bible as a basis on which his prayers were built. He taught me the secret of intercessory praying.[8]

Armin recalled,

> With this discovery, God gave me a new Bible! I had not yet learned how to make the Bible my prayer book. I began to 'dig in'. I would now search the Scriptures...meditate...mark its many promises...memorize, memorize, memorize! There are thousands of promises; a promise for every need, burden, problem, situation.[9]

"Young man," Am urged, "Learn to plead the promises of God!" Armin would say, "These words keep ringing in my soul!" As you read the Bible, underline the promises. Remember, God keeps His promises (Numbers 23:19; Hebrews 10:23; Isaiah 46:11; Psalm

89:34-36; Isaiah 30:18).

He listens to our prayer, *"For the eyes of the Lord are on the righteous and His ears are attentive to their prayer"* (1 Peter 3:12; Psalm 34:17; 1 John 5:14; 2 Chronicles 16:9; Psalm 4:4; Psalm 102:17). God not only hears, He answers our prayer, *"Before they call I will answer; while they are still speaking I will hear"* (Isaiah 65:24; Jeremiah 33:3; Mark 11:24; John 16:24; John 15:7; Isaiah 58:9; Ephesians 3:20; Matthew 7:7).

He promises to save, *"For God did not send His Son into the World to condemn it but to save the World through Him"* (John 3:17; Romans 10:9-10; 10:13; Ephesians 2:8-9; 1 Timothy 2:3-4; Hebrews 6:18).

He promises new life, *"Therefore, if anyone is in Christ he is a new creation, the old has gone the new has come!"* (2 Corinthians 5:17; John 10:10; 1 Peter 2:24; Galatians 2:20; Romans 6:4; 1 John 3:9; 2 Corinthians 3:18; Ezekiel 36:26).

He has promised liberty, *"Then you will know the Truth and the Truth will set you free…So if the Son sets you free, you will be free indeed"* (John 8:32,36; Romans 6:14,22; Romans 8:1-2; 2 Corinthians 3:17; Acts 13:38).

He has promised immunity from sin's penalty, with forthright confession, *"If we confess our sins, He is Faithful and Just and will forgive us our sins and purify us from all unrighteousness"* (1 John 1:9; Psalm 32:1-2; Isaiah 43:25; Psalm 103:12; 1 John 2:12; Ephesians 1:7; Romans 8:33).

He has promised a clean legal slate, all charges against us in the Universal Courtroom of His Holiness, dropped, *"God made Him who had no sin to be sin for us, so that in Him we might become the righteousness of God"* (2 Corinthians 5:21; Romans 8:10; 1 Corinthians 1:30; Romans 3:21-22; Romans 4:4-5; Romans 5:17). And He has promised so much more.[10]

Promises. Promises. Promises. Pray the promises. Read them, and pray them. Memorize them, and meditate on them.

God's Formula

1. Partner Petitions with Praise. Thanksgiving should not only be offered for *answers* to prayer but also for the *privilege* of prayer itself. A Hindu looks for a Brahman to do his praying for him. And then, it may not be clear to which of the million or more gods the prayer might be addressed. A Muslim does not know a tender God as Father. Allah is too transcendent to be known in such familiar terms. The idea of a personal God, touched by the feeling of our infirmities, dying for our sins, is blasphemous, too powerless to be a true god, to a Muslim. A Buddhist learns the way of suffering. He doesn't expect to be liberated from it but to be delivered to *nirvana* by suffering and death. Christians talk to God in deeply personal ways. They "cry out" to God. They complain. In fact, there is a distinct type of literature in the Old Testament called the "Complaint Psalms."[11] God cares about our complaints, few others do. These complaint psalms express hurt and doubt. Then, they often lift their heads and offer God praise.

The term *psalm* in Hebrew means the *praise*.[12] We praise God that He has given us an appointment with Him, a hearing in heaven's courtroom! What a privilege. And then we carefully wrap our requests with thanksgiving. We partner our petitions with gratitude for what God has done in the past. Never come with a fresh request without remembering God's past actions when faced with a similar problem.

2. Peer at the Problem through Grateful Eyes. Needs and pressures left unaddressed will consume us. Thanksgiving forces a fresh perspective of the problem. Thanksgiving forces us to rehearse our history with God, the history of His redemptive action. When we consciously pair every new trouble with some triumph – faith rises. "When I had this need before, God, You…" Or, "When my mother and Dad faced bankruptcy, and seemed to lose it all, you provided a new…" Or we may pray through Biblical history in the same way. "God, you did this for Israel, and you are no respecter of persons!"

Gratitude affects our attitude! And attitude, as we learned earlier, is the difference between safe landings and life crashes. No prayer request is to be offered without it being connected to some previous intervention, some record of God's goodness, or some rehearsal of God's response to a crisis. Prayer requests are suspended between blessings gratefully received and blessings anticipated.

3. Pair Praise Reports and Prayer Requests. A generation ago, in most evangelical-Pentecostal churches, prayer requests and praise reports were woven together. As some shared needs, others voiced answers to prayer – and faith rose. That model is Biblical. Wrapping a need with thanksgiving forces a view back to some moment when God answered. That triggers faith. It provides a fresh perspective in the face of our problem. Fixating on a pulsating need will only debilitate faith, inviting depression and fueling worry. Partner the need with praise. What God did in the past, He can do again. Trace the hand of God in your life and you will find fuel for faith. Confidence in God is affirmed. We are lifted out of some valley and granted a better view of God's good grace on our lives.

4. Put God in His Rightful Place – Surrender. Our culture places an emphasis on *mastering*. The Bible puts the emphasis on *being mastered* and that is the path to get out of ourselves. Jesus reminds us, we find life by losing it; we conquer by surrender; we master by serving. The process is bottom-up, others first. Narcissism tastes sweet, but in the end, it is unsavory. It is the intoxicating indulgence of self – at the center, in the spotlight, then alone, miserable, with nothing but a memory and emptiness. The greater thrill is never in the experience, but in the relationship – in self-forgetful relationships.

When Jane Adams was a little girl, she accompanied her father through the shantytown section of the city in which they lived. She was aghast, as a little girl, at the people living in "tumble-down, dilapidated shacks, crying out of their neglect." It seemed a world away. Her tender heart was forever touched. She made a declaration to her father, "Someday, Daddy, I shall build a house so big that it will take care of these people." And she did. As an adult, she went to the slums and built the big house she had envisioned as a child. She lived there, forgetting herself. She found her place in history alongside the likes of Florence Nightingale who lost herself in the suffering of soldiers.

She stands in the company of folks like Dr. Wilfred Grenfell who gave up a lucrative career as a physician to serve in far-away Labrador. He faded into anonymity and gave himself as a servant. Today, his name is on the lips of all who study the history of Labrador. Losing himself, he obtained notoriety. A missionary who labored among lepers was asked, "What is your greatest problem?" Without hesitation, he replied, "You're looking at it." Don't give God instructions – just report for duty!

5. Put Yourself on the Cross – Be Humble. Surprisingly, pride shares its throne with motley company, characters like misery and joylessness. With its close friend, resentment, pride shares an addiction to attention-getting behavior, and in the shadows, it finds itself ego-starved from a false, but sincere belief that it deserves the affirmation and compliments bestowed on another. Criticism is interpreted as an act of war since it exposes some inadequacy. Pride is not humble enough to have true friends, or to take advice, even if it is sincere. Deal with pride and self. Take up the cross. Lose your life in His. It is not the 'precious self' that needs to be eradicated, but the 'egotistical self.' After all, "a person wrapped up in himself is a pretty small package."[13] Healthy prayer helps us step outside ourselves.

Dr. E. Stanley Jones was at the end of himself. Facing a complete breakdown, he was utterly exhausted. One evening, as he concluded his speaking assignment and stepped from the platform, an inner voice spoke clearly, "Why don't you let me take over?" He recalls, that at that very moment, a crushing load of responsibilities were "instantly lifted as he gave his life utterly, wholly, completely to God." Later he would comment, "It seemed as though I walked on air that night." That experience launched the powerful ministry of the renowned E. Stanley Jones! The total surrender to God brought great power.[14]

Pride deludes us into thinking, causing us to believe we are adequate for life's problems alone. Prayer demands humility. God resists the proud and he gives grace to the humble. Prayer is founded on the promises of God, but it requires the admission that we need God's intervention. Nothing destroys pride more quickly than gratitude. Humility is fostered in a grateful heart. Pride resists gratitude. It grudgingly says, "Thank you," if at all. Pride is demanding, demeaning of others, hard and arrogant. Humility recognizes the sacrifices of others as gifts undeserved. It is tender. It empathizes and sees ourselves in the places of others. It is appreciative and empowering. A grateful person affirms others. And he sees the kindness of God.

6. Partner with Others – Don't Go it Alone. Robert Putman in his book, *Bowling Alone,* says that in the last 25 years, attendance at club meetings is down 58 percent. Families who dine together is down 33 percent. People having friends over is down 45 percent.[15] Church attendance has plummeted, by one measure by 30 percent. We are like herds of humans, who when crowded together, never talk. The preferred companionship today is electronic.

The idea of offering prayer requests is the notion that none of us dare attempt to go it alone. We need God. We need each other, and the prayers of others. Nothing draws people together more quickly than empathy with the pain and problems of each other. We are to care one for another, to pray one for another, to bear one another's burdens. Prayer for one another's needs is a declaration of our collective dependence on God. When Peter was in prison, awaiting execution, the church prayed for him. Paul requested prayer from fellow believers.

There are times when we pray for ourselves – and we should. And there are times when we cannot pray. There are times when pressures and burdens may have laid us so low that we need someone else to pray for us and with us. Pride keeps us from requesting prayer. A prayer request is never an excuse to solicit others to do the hard work of personal prayer for us. The point is that we are not to travel alone. We are devoted to one another's success (Romans 12:10). We encourage (2 Corinthians 13:11) and edify one another (1 Thessalonians 4:18), and prayer (James 5:16) is a means to that end. We minister one to another through prayer.

During the invasion of Guam in WW II, Donald Vairin was a hospital corpsman. His boat hit a coral reef and came to a grinding stop in the water. Everyone was ordered overboard. Donald jumped into the water without thinking and sank like a rock, pulled down by the weight of his carbine rifle, medical pack, canteen and boots. He was fighting for his life. He struggled upward to the surface, gasping for air and then sank again. Treading water, he was trying to rid himself of his boots and weighty paraphernalia. Exhausted, he felt that he was at the end.

Suddenly, another soldier was next to him, thrashing wildly. In desperation, he grabbed hold of him and managed to stay afloat. Together, they got to a reef and a rescue boat pulled them both on board to safety. Donald recalls the guilt about clutching onto the fellow soldier to save himself. He never apologized for potentially endangering his life. He never admitted his own fear. On shore leave in San Francisco, six months later, he happened into a restaurant. A uniformed sailor spotted him and heralded him to his table and announced to his friends, "This is my buddy. He saved my life." Donald said in disbelief, "What are you talking about?" The Navy boy countered, "Don't you remember? We were in the water together at Guam. You grabbed onto me. I was going down, and you held me up." The two struggling soldiers, both drowning, had kept each other alive. Who actually saved the other?[16] *"Woe to him who is alone when he falls. When one falls, the other will lift up his fellow"* (Ecclesiastes 4:10).

7. Pray with Others – Form a Prayer Covenant Group. The late Evelyn Christenson declared emphatically,

> When people start praying together...things begin to change. Our lives change, our families change, our churches change, our communities change. A family altar can alter the family, and a church praying together transforms the church. Changes take place, not when we study about prayer, not when we talk about it, not even when we memorize beautiful Scripture verses on prayer; it is when we actually pray that things begin to happen.[17]

This interdependence of the body is a critical part of our survival. We agree with one another in prayer (Mt. 18:19-20) and find people who will touch God and the solution to our dilemma in prayer. Unified prayer is a powerful thing (Acts 4:31). As we take on the burdens of others in prayer, we express our deep love for one another. Their pain brings tears to us. Their problem produces travail in us. Much of the world, if it only knew, would die to be a part of such a fellowship.

8. Prayer Over One Another – Gather for Prayer. Many times, at a Prayer Summit, I have seen a burdened soul break free from pride and come to the seat in the middle of a circle of dozens of fellow pastors. At first, there is often silence. Then tears. At times, there is a gasp at the recognition of a need so grave that Goliath himself might be a welcome reprise. As the individual prays his need, often disclosing for the first time outside his family, something very personal, everyone in the room suddenly feels themselves sitting in the chair with their needy peer. Poignant, empathetic prayers pour forth, often ripe with unconscious prophetic insights. Scriptures are fervently read or quoted. One prays and then another. One man kneels at the feet of the wounded supplicant; others may stand with a hand on the shoulder. It is as if a trained group of surgeons is tending the person. The Holy Spirit is at work. At times sagging shoulders straighten. A drooped chin rises. Tired arms reach out and up as if Christ was physically present in the room. The burden is being lifted. Tears of grief give way to tears of joy. The great exchange is taking place.

A Practical Formula – Remodel Prayer Request Time. We need the opportunity to "request prayer" from friends. Too often, however, our prayer request time is a barrage of needs about which no one prays fervently or specifically. Burdens are not lifted. Breakthroughs rarely occur. What we need are special venues for prayer that do not fit neatly into our slick and quick Sunday morning services. Instead of a dizzying number of prayer needs soon forgotten, or a printed list with so many items we are overwhelmed, we have to learn to slow down our prayer times, to be patient and selective. Instead of prayer models designed to allow us to hand-off our personal needs and requests to others, we should be involved in the prayer. At times, we should labor over one another, one need at a time, and wrestle in prayer in behalf of a discouraged soul, remembering that the presenting need is rarely the more critical need. The underlying need is often intangible – faith, lack of optimism, attitude issues, a sense of being cared for, the feeling of being alone with a hardship that growls like a tiger and snaps like an alligator. Hearing a cacophony of fervent voices, all praying for our need, and feeling the caring circle around us, seeing the tears of others in our behalf – causes faith to rise. We are not alone with the problem. After all, others now know. They have entered into our battle. This is huge. This is not merely psychological – the Spirit bears witness with the Word. It is as if the witnesses that line the balcony of heaven shout hope at us from the pages of Scripture. They made it to heaven's shores, so can we. "God is no respecter of persons!"

In too many churches, if there is a prayer request time, so many needs pour forth and so little time is allotted that intercession cannot occur in any meaningful way. We splash lists on a screen with dozens of scrolling names and needs – deaths, hospitalizations, accidents and injuries, medical tests, relationship challenges. The opposite of faith occurs. Deprivation and overload result. In a sea of painful information, we feel overwhelmed. People with genuine needs hardly feel cared for as a result of such an impersonal experience. Their precious and poignant needs are only a small part of a parade of pain to which the church inadequately responds. Bearing one another's burdens in prayer is a highly personal and relational thing. When reduced to mere fact, to a numbered need, we depersonalize the petition and the person, and the consequence is less passion. The piles of prayer requests on the tables of televangelists are hardly what Paul had in mind. We are to 'pray one for another' in the context of caring relationships. Prayer is relational. The more impersonal it is, the more it is distorted from its Biblical norm.

Create Unhurried Seasons for Prayer. A generation ago, altar time at the conclusion of a Sunday service was a time for extended prayer by the entire congregation in many congregations. Most, if not all, came forward to find a place near the pulpit, near the place from which the Scripture was heralded. They knelt. They poured out their hearts in petition. Passionate prayer was common, mixed with tears and heart-felt cries. After some season, those who continued to wrestle in prayer could expect that others would kneel next to them, as concerned brothers or sisters, and pray. Some knew the need. Others prayed with the leading of the Spirit. Such prayer expected the seeker to tarry until victory was assured, and the person rose with shouts of joy and a settled sense of peace.

Prayers can be short and still be effective! Elijah's prayer was about sixty words – in English, some twenty-to-thirty seconds of sound. The prophets of Baal had prayed all day without an answer. Elijah prayed his brief prayer – and the fire fell (I Kings 18:36-37). And yet, there times when prayer is likened to travail. It is intense and lingering. It seizes your whole being – and there is nothing else to do but pray (Galatians 4:19). In such moments, prayer is the only thing on the agenda!

Claim Christ's Victory through Prayer. Wesley Duewel declares,

> Christ has chosen to rule the world through prayer...Christ is already enthroned at the right hand of the Father. What is He doing? He is reigning. But how is He reigning? Not by His scepter, but by prayer. Even before His resurrection, when He forewarned Peter that Satan had asked permission to sift the disciples as wheat (Luke 22:31-32), Christ did not say, 'I will stop Satan.' Instead, He said, 'I have prayed for you.'[18]

Christ reigns, Duewel argues, through prayer.

When John, "in the Spirit" on the Lord's Day is invited through the open door of prayer to gain a glimpse of heaven, what he sees is stunning, breathtaking. God is on His throne and sharing it is the lion-like Lamb, Christ Himself. Around the throne of God are 24 other thrones for the elders of heaven who serve in some mysterious way, as custodians of prayers to which God has said, "Yes, but not yet!" They hold bowls of incense, as if our prayers have taken on a

146

material and fragrant form. The atmosphere is one of resilient and triumphant worship. It is clear, the requests held by these elders, prayed by God's people on the earth, have not strained the resources of heaven. No one is working furiously to assure earth's need. Prayer here is mixed with worshipful praise.

The state of earth's needs are subsumed by the sound of triumph. Each elder has a kingly crown, denoting authority. So prayer and authority here are conjoined. The custodians of prayer reign as kings. They are seated, enthroned. Prayer rules. They are both priestly (prayerfully, worshipful) and yet kingly (crowns and authority). Ah, but they cast their crowns before the throne in deference to God's sovereignty. Prayer must always do that. Authority is derived. We reign in Christ, but our crowns are subordinate to His. Our dominion flows to and from His authority. Simultaneously, the elders mix fire from the altar in heaven and release flaming incense into the earth. Incense has no fragrance until it is touched by fire. Prayer without fire is always lacking. On the earth side, we only feel the heat of some fiery trial. Hold on. Heaven is sending the sound and sweet smell of certain victory. From heaven, God rules by prayer.

In the Revelation, the burning of incense, prayer, and the opening of the seals on the scroll of redemption that reclaim the earth as belonging to the Lamb are bound together. Somehow, as we pray – the seals that reveal and assert God's authority over this planet are broken. Mysteriously, prayer, linked to the right of Christ regained by the cross, strengthens heaven's grip on the earth. In heaven, prayer and authority fuse together by the redemptive work of Christ. Revelation comes. Authority increases. Heaven is rejoicing, but John was weeping. No one was able to open the scroll.

"Weep not, for the lion of the tribe of Judah has prevailed to open the book and lose the seals on the scroll." The scroll is the title deed to the earth itself, the certification that "the earth is Lord's" – twice his.

147

First, by creation and then by redemption. God is not planning to abandon the earth, quite the opposite. The 'world' is not our home, but the earth is – in fact, heaven is coming to the earth. The New Jerusalem will descend to the earth and it will be made new. We were created for the earth. We, through our relationship with Christ, have a legal right to it. We are called to steward it, to guard it, to cultivate and to serve in it as agents of the kingdom of God.

Shout after Prayer. It is not God's intent that we remain silent about answers to prayer. The provision of God and fresh answers to prayer are evidences of his benevolent and watchful character. Our silence about such interventions is a missed opportunity for evangelism. When heaven opens doors and divine favor is apparent, we are presented with bragging moments about the goodness of God. "Look what the Lord has done! He's alive. I prayed, and he answered." And, we whisper to our friend, "What He did for me, He will do for you." To miraculously see a negative problem turn positive and attribute it to chance, after we have specifically prayed about it, is abominable faith. With such practices, answers to prayer dry up. God wants us to give thanks, and not just in church, but before skeptical friends and family.

Let's review. We pull down heaven's joy. We rejoice, always. We keep our poise before a watching world. We cultivate a sense of expectancy (the imminence of His return), and the immediacy of his presence. And we refuse to worry – a self-imposed prohibition. Prohibitions are difficult. When children are told, "Don't think about candy or ice cream, it is precisely what they think about!" The prohibition, left to itself, ratchets up the impulse to think about what we are not to think about. So Paul adds an offensive strategy. We win the battle by pushing back at the problem and turning toward God. Pray. Be Supple. Give thanks.

Tell Your Story – Play Your Music

Mother Teresa once said, "Joy is a net of love by which you can catch souls."[19] We should never hear from heaven and remain silent. We overcome with the word of our testimony. Our declarations of anticipated victory are especially significant. Then, when answers come, that public testimony of hope is remembered – and faith rises in the hearts of hearers.

God answers our prayers not merely to relieve our pain. Our lives are his billboard to advertise both the reality of his existence and his caring nature. He is alive. He hears. He answers. He cares. He is a good God. In fact, God is short for 'good.' God is a synonym for unbounded goodness. *"His mercy endures forever!"* (Psa. 136). *"His compassions fail not"* (Lam. 3:22). When we have prayed, and a solution has come, how dare we keep silent? And when it has not come, still, we sing – as a declaration of faith in the character of God.

George Frideric Handel was to offer an oratorio, but the hall was nearly empty. Promoters were apologetic. "Never mind," the great musician replied, "The music will sound the better." Handel knew that the acoustics of an empty hall were so different than one packed with people. His friends were about the crowds, the people, but he was all about the music.[20] Mother Teresa said, "It doesn't matter what you do. It only matters how much love you put into what you do." Don't wait for a full house and a stage. Perform for an audience of One. Sing. Shout praise.

REVIEW It

1. "Call unto me, and I will _____."
2. Gratitude affects our _____.
3. The term "psalm" means _____.
4. _____ is important as a first step in asking for help from God.

5. Woe to him who is _____ when he falls.

TALK About It

1. Prayer is not magic. God is not a genie. Prayer is not something always answered if we "pray just right" as if by some formula or method – that, in fact, is a pagan idea. True or false?

2. Talk about prayer requests, not as information, but in reference to relationships.

3. Do you think we want "God" or merely "help" from God?

4. We place an emphasis on mastering. God puts the emphasis on being mastered – discuss the difference.

5. If God told you today, he would answer no more prayer requests, would you continue to serve him? If another *faith* system offered you more of what you want and need, would you switch?

Endnotes

1. Charles H. Gabriel, *My Father Watches Over Me* (The Rodeheaver Co.: Renewed, 1938).

2. Mike MacIntosh. *Falling in Love with Prayer* (Colorado Springs, CO: Victor Books, 2004), 27.

3. John Julian, editor; *A Dictionary of Hymnology: Setting Forth the Origin and History of Christian Hymns; "When God Inclines the Heart to Pray,"* (New York: Charles Scribner's Sons, 1892), 907; From Spurgeon's O. O. H. Bk, 1866.

4. Margaret Poloma and George Gallup, Jr., *Varieties of Prayer* (Philadelphia, PA: Trinity Press International, 1991), 26-52.

5. Mike MacIntosh. *Falling in Love with Prayer* (Colorado Springs, CO: Victor Books, 2004), 17-18.

6. Eddie Smith. *How To Be Heard in Heaven* (Minneapolis, MN: Bethany House, 2007), 56.

7. www.global24-7.org/downloads/The%20promises%20of%20 God.pdf.

8. Quoted by D.L. Moody. See www.jwipn.com/pdf/Pray%20 The%20Promises%20of%20God.pdf.

9. Ibid.

10. He has promised the Holy Spirit (Luke 11:13; Isaiah 44:3; John 14:16-17; John 16:7; Acts 1:8; Acts 2:38-39 Galatians 4:6; Galatians 3:14; 1; John 4:13; Matthew 3:11; Ezekiel 36:27; Ephesians 1:13). He has pledged to protect us from the Evil One (2 Thessalonians 3:3; 2 Timothy 4:18; Colossians 1:13; Colossians 2:15; 1 John 5:18; Romans 8:38,39; Psalm 91:9-13; Hebrews 2:14-15), and to be present with us (Matthew 28:20; Isaiah 43:5; James 4:8; John 14:15-16; Matthew 18:20; Psalm 23:4; Hebrews 13:5). He has pledged His love (Romans 5:8; Jeremiah 31:3), joy (John 15:11) and peace (Isaiah 53:5) as well as hope (Romans 15:4). Eternal life is a promise (1 John 2:25; Romans 6:23). He is coming again (Acts 1:11; 1 Thessalonians 4:16-17). There is a heaven (Revelation 21:2-3) in our future, and power in our present (Isaiah 40:29; Psalm 29:11). We can trust God (Proverbs 3:25-26). He will give us wisdom (Ecclesiastes 2:26). He will teach us (Psalm 25:8 – 10) and guide us (Isaiah 30:21). He wants us to be successful (Joshua 1:8; 2 Chronicles 20:20) and our plans to succeed (Psalm 20:4). In times of difficulty, He will comfort us (Matthew 5:4). He blesses the house of the righteous (Proverbs 3:33), and promises health (Jeremiah 30:17; Deuteronomy 7:12, 15) and protection (1 Samuel 2:9; Psalm 125: 1-2). He will meet our needs (Philippians 4:19; Matthew 6:25-26,31-33), and does not want us to walk in fear and doubt ((Isaiah 41:10; 41:13). For times of depression (Psalm 43:5) or failure and trouble (John 14:1; Psalm 37; 73), or anxiety (Philippians 4:6-7; Matthew 6:30, 34), He has given us promises. When Satan comes against us, we have promises for the moment (1 Corinthians 10:13; 2 Peter 2:7-9). When fleshly enemies assail, we have His promises (1 Peter 1:4-7; Jeremiah 15:21; Psalm 27:1-2). He gives power for His service (Zechariah 4:6; Acts.1:8). And the promise of provision (Luke 12:24; Philippians 4:19; Psalm 84:11-12).

11. Communal Complaint Psalms are 44; 58; 60; 74; 79; 80; 83; 106; 125. They usually include calling Yahweh by name. Then, lamenting over some misfortune, followed by a plea to God to transform the misfortune. Additionally, there are sometimes thoughts intended to inspire confidence to believe that God will respond, or to move Him to action, by appealing, for example, to His honor or His name. They usually end with an affirmation of being heard – a conclusive "resting" in anticipation of a response. Complaint psalms may be on the occasion of a national fast. They may be in response to some catastrophe or disaster, war or pestilence, famine

or a plague. There are also Individual Complaint Psalms. They are Psalms 3; 5; 6; 7; 13; 17; 22; 25; 26; 27:7-14; 28; 31; 35; 38; 39; 42-43; 54-57; 59; 61; 63; 64; 69; 70; 71; 86; 88; 102; 109; 120; 130; 140; 141; 142; 143. Indeed, the Bible is full of the record of people complaining to God. These individual laments follow basically the same order as above. The summons to God. The complaint or lament. The invitation for God to intervene – for His honor, because of the threats of the enemy, or by the nature of the situation. The petition or plea is the heart of the psalm. It is sometimes referred to as an entreaty implying that the basis of appeal is due to some violation of the treaty or covenant. Something is not as it was intended to be. God must keep His part of the bargain. Or, man must recognize his failure, in which case, there are confessional petitions. And also, petitions of innocence. There is finally the expressed conviction that the plea was heard, and heaven will answer. At times, there is the pledge of a vow.

12. H. C. G. Moule. *Studies in Philippians* (Grand Rapids, MI: Kregel; 1977), 113.

13. Martin H. Manser, *The Westminster Collection Of Christian Quotations* (Westminster: John Knox Press, 2001), 338.

14. Alan Axelrod, *Winston Churchill, CEO: 25 Lessons for Bold Business Leaders* (New York: Sterling Publishing Company, 2009), 78-79.

15. Quoted by Robert Foster, 161.

16. Morgan, 135-136; Adapted from Donald Vairin, *His Mysterious Ways* (Guideposts, September, 1999), 39.

17. Evelyn Christenson, Quoted by Elizabeth Key, 66.

18. Wesley Duewel, *Touch the World Through Prayer* (Zondervan, 1986), 39-40.

19. Teresa (Mother), José Luis González-Balado, Janet N. Playfoot, *My Life for the Poor* (Harper & Row, 1985), 37.

20. Morgan, *More Stories*, 108.

REVIEW It Answers

1. Answer
2. Attitude
3. Praise
4. Thanksgiving
5. Alone

Why should I feel discouraged,
why should the shadows come,
Why should my heart be lonely,
and long for heaven and home,
When Jesus is my portion –
My constant friend is He:
His eye is on the sparrow,
and I know He watches me;
His eye is on the sparrow,
and I know He watches me.
"Let not your heart be troubled,"
His tender word I hear,
And resting on His goodness,
I lose my doubts and fears;
Though by the path He leadeth,
but one step I may see;
His eye is on the sparrow,
and I know He watches me;
His eye is on the sparrow,
and I know He watches me.
Whenever I am tempted,
whenever clouds arise,
When songs give place to sighing,
when hope within me dies,
I draw the closer to Him,
from care He sets me free;
His eye is on the sparrow,
and I know He watches me;
His eye is on the sparrow,
and I know He watches me.

Chorus
I sing because I'm happy,
I sing because I'm free,
For His eye is on the sparrow,
And I know He watches me. [1]

CHAPTER ELEVEN
Step Nine: Make the Great Exchange

Let your moderation be made known to all men...
let your requests be made known to God.

Perspective: Far too often, prayer request time is a litany of woes. Everyone feels worse after the experience than before and those offering a prayer request are no better for the experience. They come and go depressed, joyless and pained. Such moments are not typically windows of hope for a watching world. Suppose it were different. Suppose the same people detailed the same problem, but with radiant faces, footnoting their problems with memories from past divine interventions.

Suppose they thanked God for the privilege of prayer itself, and expressed confidence, not superficially, about the goodness of God and their faith that He would hear and answer. Suppose in that moment, you saw an almost visible transformation – a people laden down with cares were suddenly overcome, as by some magical spell, by a resolute and sincere joy and peace. Weighed down physically and emotionally, you witnessed an uncanny resilience reflected in their very demeanor. Mourning gave way to dancing. Heaviness to hope. You ask, "What is happening to these people?" You have just watched "the Great Exchange."

There are so many awards these days that awards have almost lost their meaning. Some honors are to be treasured. Some are to be avoided like the black plague. The annual "Darwin Awards" honor people who killed themselves in ridiculous ways – the disabled man, obviously in more than one way, who grew impatient with the closed elevator door and drove his scooter into it, not once, but three times, finally crashing the door open and sending him plummeting 40 feet down into the shaft, scooter and all. He received the award posthumously. Or, the man who lit a torch to weld a new handle onto the heavy *soil tamper* the family had used for years, none of them knowing that it was actually a loaded cannon shell. Through those many years, family members, ignorantly and naively, one, then another banged the loaded cannon shell on the ground, not realizing it was an explosive. Miracuously they had lived, but this was too much. Fire ignited the powder and it exploded. The poor man obviously did not know the bang that was in the 'soil tamper'. And there is the story of the man, desperate and poor, who decided to commit a robbery. For a mask, he spray-painted his face gold! Loaded down with merchandise and leaving the crime scene, his body reacted to the toxins in the paint. He suffered a respiratory attack and died. Successful – at what? Someone has cynically said, "It may be that your sole purpose in life is to be a warning to others." Surely that is not God's plan for you.

Nobodies to Somebodies

Most of us learned first, not of Pharaoh, but of Moses. Pharaoh had it all. Moses was the nobody, but God takes nobodies and makes somebodies of them. Certainly Pharaoh is important to history, archaeology and museum collectors. But few people read his decrees or live by the principles he recorded. Moses, the nobody, is a contributor to the most read book of history. His legal code is the foundation for western law. Our lives are informed by values he scribbled down on the top of Mount Sinai. They are still the guiding moral foundation for much of the earth.

Hannah was a lonely housewife, a nobody, but in prayer her barrenness was transformed, and her son Samuel reset the moral thermostat of the nation and united the disparate tribes, forging them into one nation. He then anointed and mentored a young shepherd who would become Israel's greatest king, David. He, too, was a nobody, not even invited by his own father to be reviewed by the prophet as a 'somebody'. Instead, alone, he fought off lions and bears to fend for the sheep. He was constantly placed in harm's way and treated with less respect than a servant. But God saw his heart and chose him to be the king.

Key Principle

Suppose people detailed some problem, but with radiant faces, with memories from past divine interventions. Suppose they thanked God and expressed confidence in the goodness of God. Suppose you saw an almost visible transformation - a people laden down with care, suddenly overcome, as by some magical spell, by a resolute and sincere joy and peace. You witnessed an uncanny resilience. Mourning gave way to dancing. Heaviness to hope. You have just watched *the Great Exchange.*

Like the Bible greats, before God, we pour out our pain. But before men, we maintain our poise, act in measured and moderate ways, and lift up voices that reflect joy and thanksgiving. Before God, we detail our needs. We may weep. We may passionately plead. We may sob. We may reveal our broken heart. Before men, we delight in God's promises. We shout for joy. We refuse to allow the enemy to silence us. We wait for God's provision. This is not duplicity. It is not hypocrisy. It is faith in action; faith over feelings; faith over worldly facts in view of heaven's promises. It is an expression of confidence in God. It is a reflection of trust in the Lord. It is a bold declaration that we believe God has heard and He will answer. It is subversive action, against the norm, against the pain, against the poverty, the want, the need, the debilitating situation. It is the sound of an alternative reality. It is evidence of the nearness of God – of His protection and provision, of His power and presence. This is the Great Exchange. The right to petition demands this exchange. For such a privilege, how could we do anything else?

Dr. John Sarno is a professor of rehabilitative medicine at the New York University School of Medicine. His specialty is back pain. Decades ago, he began to see a fascinating data contradiction. The levels of pain reported by patients were not supported by physical evidence, and yet, what followed was very real degeneration. He challenged conventional wisdom, and soon discovered that the back pain had less to do with physical injury, job strain and the like, and more to do with the invisible burdens carried by the people. A whopping 88 percent of those with chronic back pain had a history of tension-induced reactions. The pain radiated into their heads in the form of tension and migraine headaches. It affected their vitals with colitis and ulcers. It manifested in their respiratory tract with asthma and hay fever. It created weeping skin. Stiff shoulders and neck pain were common. Aching sensations in the legs were possible. All from back pain and spasms, the body shouting because of the invisible burden it was carrying.[2] "Emotions do not lie," Dr. Don Colbert says, "We bury them, but we are burying something that is still living."[3]

The God Who Acts

"If you ask anything in My name, I will do it!" (John 14:14). *"I*

will do it!" Not, "I will help you. I will be your partner." Or, "I will enable you to do it." Or even, "I will make you stronger and more confident." He says, *"I will do it!"* Some things, no doubt, He enables and empowers us to do. He does work through human agency. He does call us to partner with Him. But, there are times when He wants us to unload the whole weight of some humanly impossible problem onto Him in prayer. And then, in the face of that mountain, shout for joy! Five things urge God to act.

1. Know God. The first character you meet in the Bible is God. He is acting. And He is acting in history in a demonstrable, visible way. In Genesis, he speaks into the darkness reordering the chaotic world. He creates from nothing. He blesses Adam and Eve, and then conveys the power of blessing. The Sovereign of sovereigns, he gave 'dominion' to Adam, not holding the reigns so tightly that he did not share authority. He endows humanity in His image, literally, His shadow. He fashions man as human through flesh and blood, a creature of earth, but with a divine imprint bearing His likeness, patterned after Him. He is a God who acts – benevolently. A life-giving, authority-sharing God, who is on one hand infinite, past finding out, beyond comprehension. And on the other hand, one who walks through the garden in the cool of the day, wanting the companionship of man.

He is a blue collar Regent. A working God. Self-disclosing. Simultaneously, holy and humble; just and merciful. Familiar as a Father, and yet as infinite as Father Time and abstract space. What a God. He can be known. Yet, He can never be fully known. Talk to Him. No, be silent before Him. Run to Him. He loves you. No, fear and reverence Him. Fall down before Him. One name is not adequate. Throughout Scripture, He reveals different facets of Himself, using different names – *Yahweh Jireh,* the Provider; *Yahweh Nissi* – the War Banner; *Yahweh Ro'i* – the Shepherd; *Yahweh Shammah* – the

Lord, there in Jerusalem; *Yahweh M'Kaddish* – the Sanctifier; *Yahweh Rapha* – the Healer; *Yahweh Shalom* – Peace; *Yeshua* – Salvation; *Adonai* – Master, Lord; and more.

2. Know Who You Are in God. From the Mount of Olives, looking south, one can see a cone-shaped mountain, about three miles southeast of Bethlehem, irregular in symmetry. It is the Herodium. It is a man-made mountain, built by Herod in order to create a high point at which a signal from Masada might be seen and relayed to his fortress in Jerusalem. To create the volcano-shaped mountain, Herod ordered one mountain moved and placed on top of the other. Bit-by-bit, and shovel-by-shovel, the mountain was moved. Herod had ordered it. To such power Jesus says, *"If you have faith like a mustard seed, you shall say to this mountain, 'Remove from this place to that,' and it will remove; and nothing shall be impossible to you"* (Matthew 17:20). Jesus was urging His disciples, who were intimidated by Herod's power, to believe that an even greater power was at their disposal. Herod spoke to a mountain, and the force of his office moved it by the strength of an army of laborers. The disciples, too, would speak, and the force of their faith would move mountains. The Scripture urges – *"Be honest in your estimate of yourselves, measuring your value by how much faith God has given you"* (Romans 12:3, TLB). He wants us to have great faith.

3. Know that He Believes in You. Jesus believed in His disciples. They were common men – fishermen, a tax collector, a political zealot, tradesmen, common and uneducated – but He trusted His entire effort on earth into their hands. At Pentecost, they would be called *ignorant and unlearned,* but with the power of the Holy Spirit, they would turn the world upside down. Thomas Edison was branded by a schoolmaster as "retarded." As a result, he only finished three months of formal education.[4] An elementary teacher wrote off Albert Einstein. Having the approval of the world is not always a sign of success.

4. Know that His Will is Best. "...*If we ask anything according to His will, He hears us. And if we know that He hears us, whatever we ask, we know that we have the petitions that we have asked of Him*" (1 John 5:14-15, NKJV). Every flight demands a flight plan that is on file with air traffic control. Every 30 days, to be legal, a pilot must update his *approach* data which informs his flight plan. New skyscrapers and towers go up all the time. Airports expand and add runways. The approaches are constantly altered. The *attitude* of the plane – nose up – never changes. But the *approach* constantly changes, and so with us. Recently, the silence in the cockpit of a friend, quietly cruising at 9,000 feet in route to his destination, was broken. He responded and identified himself. The controller informed him that his course was being changed and he was to copy the new coordinates. Suddenly, and without an apparent cause to him, he had to chart a new course. There was no dialogue. There were no multiple choice options – just a command. He would fly to a specific aeronautical intersection, though invisible, and then to another, and from that point, latitude and longitude coupled with altitude, he would make his airport, runway approach. There was no negotiation with the tower. No, "I've filed my flight plan, and I am sticking with it." No, "Look, other planes can dodge me – I am not altering my course for the big birds." He would learn later, his current course was taking him into a sea of thunderheads. He would be surrounded on three sides, walled in by the angry clouds, full of lightning. The controller was trying to save his little plane – and his life. We should make our best plans, keep our radio on, and if we hear from heaven's tower, be ready to change directions and approaches. God knows best. Pray for his will.

5. Know that He is No Respecter of Persons. William Bennett is a professor of physics at Yale University. He has done the calculation. He claims that a trillion monkeys sitting in front of computers, typing 10 characters per second, 80-100 words per minute, and doing so for a trillion times longer than the Universe has existed, would not produce the line, "To be or not to be. That is the question." Count the letters and the spaces. Approximately the same odds should exist for this line, *"God so loved _____ [insert your name], that He gave His only Son."* A prayer life will not advance very far if you are praying to a God whose love for you, you doubt. If you are convinced God would do thus and so for another but not for you, go back to the cross and settle the issue of His love for you. Exempting yourself from the reach of His grace is deadly to a prayer life.

6. Know His Word and Promises. Knowing the will of God, discerning the voice of God, is not a mechanical thing. It is not a technique. First, it demands knowledge of God's Word. Your mind is renewed as you pull down imaginations and thought patterns informed by the flesh and the world, and replace them with a Biblical world view. But this is more than facts. It is knowledge of God Himself, a what-would-Jesus-do awareness and that demands a relationship, one informed by the Spirit and the Word.

Prayer God Answers

1. Ask. God knows what you need, but He demands that you ask! It is a mystery. *"You have not, because you ask not!"* (James 4:2) Have you ever noticed that Jesus rarely took the initiative in miracles? He typically waited for people to approach Him. At times, they chased Him down, yelled to gain His attention, tore open roofs or pressed toward Him through crowded streets. They overcame the objections of others and the obstacles in their way. They were desperate to get to Him. Ask.

We are to ask in His name (John 14:13-14; 15:16; 16:23, 24, 26). We are to ask that the Father may be glorified in connection with the Son (John 14:12-14). We are to ask according to His will

(John 15:7-8). We are to ask anything (John 16:23). We are to be persistent in prayer, determined, to ask and keep on asking. If you "have not," ask God.

2. Ask Sincerely. Prayer, to be effective and receive an answer, must also be sincere – it must be pure in motive. It must be without pretense. There cannot be hidden and ulterior motives. God does not honor duplicitous praying. He wants us to be straightforward with Him. And prayer must generally be sensible. God made the sun stand still once, but it isn't something He chooses to do every day. There are exceptions, but asking for snow in August is usually a futile request unless you live in Alaska.

It was a Friday night, and the high school team was seriously behind. Heads were hanging low. The coach grabbed the face mask of an under-performing lineman, "What's the matter with you?" The big boy said, "Coach, I am saving myself for the next game." The coach exploded, "Next game? Next game! There is no next game. There is only this game here and now."[5] Get real. Be sincere.

3. Ask with Passion. Prayer demands heart. It was the second season for Lou Holtz as head football coach of Notre Dame, the fighting Irish. The team had just experienced a humiliating defeat at the hands of Texas A & M in the Cotton Bowl. Coach Holtz entered the post-game locker room dejected, only to discover that his players were not distraught. His blood pressure rose. There wasn't any fight in the 'Fightin' Irish,' with one exception. Chris Zorich, a second stringer, sat in front of his locker sobbing. Holtz did not forget the moment. The next year, he set out to build a different team, one composed of players who loved the game as much as he and Chris Zorich loved it. Chris went from a second string sub, to a starter, and then to team captain. He helped Lou Holtz and the Fighting Irish win a national championship. It was not the talent of Zorich that won him a starting spot, but his heart, his tears, his passion. Some things are worth crying over.

Martin R. DeHaan, the great Bible teacher believed, "A tear is a distillation of the soul. It is the deepest longing of the human heart in chemical solution." Spurgeon called tears "the diamonds of heaven." Golda Meir, the Prime Minister of Israel would argue, "Those who don't know how to weep with their whole heart, don't know how to laugh either." Tears are our body's way of washing out toxic chemicals that accumulate in times of emotional distress. Manganese affects our moods. When we shed tears, the level of manganese discharged is 30 times that found in our blood. The lachrymal gland not only determines the flow of tears, but also concentrates and removes the excess manganese from the body. With the toxins gone, we see better – through tears.[6] Folks suffering with psoriasis and eczema are sometimes "weeping through their skin", the body crying or exploding like an inner silent volcano, pushing to the surface the toxins. Some are unable to weep openly. So the body finds a way to discharge the negative pent-up energy.[7]

4. Ask According to the Word. Prayer should be premised on Scripture, on the promises of the Word. It should be prayed in and with the power of the Holy Spirit. The best praying is when you are not praying alone, but when you are praying as a part of divine partnership. Your prayers should have a kingdom perspective, and not merely be a selfish whim. They should seek to be an expression of the will of God, to further His kingdom purposes and to glorify Jesus Christ. Faith is demanded. Without faith, God does not hear. This is faith not only in the ability of God, but a surrendered trust to His will and way. Finally, it is good to remember that "God takes the route that brings Him the most glory...And, on its way to better, it may drop by worse."[8]

5. Ask with the Enabling of the Spirit. The Holy Spirit works with us in our praying. He invites us to pray, drawing us closer to

God (Revelation 22:17). He sanctifies us, qualifying us to pray and our prayers as answerable (1 Peter 1:2). He prepares us for praying and then enables us to pray (John 16:13, 14). He, Himself, communicates through us, and instructs us for effective praying (Romans 8:26). He reveals things to us, assuring us (I Corinthians 2:9, 10). He consoles us, inspiring us (Acts 9:31). He joins our intercession, partnering with us, guiding us in prayer (Jude 20, 21). He raises the level of our expectancy, sustaining us all the while (Romans 8:23). He helps us pray. He perfects our imperfect pleas. He prays for us and through us and in us. He is the Helper who helps us pray.

6. Ask with a Pure Heart. *"Thou shall not steal!"* It seems rather straight-forward – no fine print, no hidden clauses, no room for misinterpretation. Yet, the Jewish people developed 2,748 commentaries on this one phrase. They had at least 4,801 different interpretations of the meaning of the commandment, and 5,000 exceptions, rendering the simple law impotent.[9] To pray, with purity of heart, demands honesty and integrity before God. When we are down to the bottom of our barrel, we do our best praying.

7. Ask in the Name. The issue is not only praying in His name, but living in His name! Glibly uttering the syllables "Gee-sus!" is hardly praying in the name of "Jesus!" Some folks might as well say, "Shazam!" Sounds do not fool God or manipulate spirits. To pray by the authority encoded in the name of Jesus is to pray in harmony with and to be sanctioned to use the badge of His name. Crooked cops can flaunt their badges, but both the ethically straight-laced and the sleazy know that the authority is being flashed around in a frivolous and phony way. In effect, it is no authority at all.

There is a veritable war against the name of Jesus in our nation today. "There is no other name…" Why does the world so hate Jesus – a healer, a teacher of incomparable moral values, a crusader for the rejected and hopeless? He never advocated violence, never acted as the aggressor, never justified revolution, paid His taxes, and lived as a model citizen. Everything God wants to give is bound up in His name. We pray – in His name. Experience miracles – in His name. Sustain the weary – in His name. Liberate the oppressed – in His name. See souls saved – in His name. There is no other name!

8. Ask in Faith. Before faith exerts its control over circumstances, it is intended to control us in the middle of circumstances. If faith can anchor, it will keep us whether the circumstances change or not. There is *delivering* faith. But there is also *sustaining* faith – and both are treated equally before God. Hebrews 11 declares that the ancients *"subdued kingdoms, worked righteousness, obtained promises, stopped the mouths of lions, quenched the violence of fire, escaped the edge of the sword, out of weakness were made strong, became valiant in battle and turned to flight the armies of the aliens."* Then seamlessly, the writer of Hebrews declares,

> *Others were tortured, not accepting deliverance, that they might obtain a better resurrection. Still others had trials of mockings and scourgings, yes, and of chains and imprisonment. They were stoned, they were sawn in two, were tempted, were slain with the sword. They wandered about in goatskins, being destitute, afflicted, tormented...*

Of them, *"the world was not worthy."* Yet, there is no distinction between these groups. No *Class One Faith,* and *Class Two.* *"All these...obtained a good testimony through faith..."* (Hebrews 11:33-39). Faith is mostly about being faithful. Some, He delivers from. Others, He delivers through. Still others, He delivers to Himself. Leave the decision to Him. Commit to be faithful. Job's radical declaration rings forth, *"Though He slay me, yet will I trust in Him"* (Job 1:4-5; 13:15). True prayer is a way of life, not merely a panic call during an emergency.

Those who ask God for some miracle, some breakthrough, some

provision – and give up when it does not come through are not evidencing faith. Faith is anchored to God's character as much as it is to His ability. It is more about *His* benevolent and sovereign will, not to our will imposed on Him. Do we trust Him? Do we have faith in His character? Will we press on, though heaven seems silent?

Explain the Problem to God

"Let your requests be made known" is a call to detail our needs. We are to articulate them, describe them. Tell God the problem. Give thanks for His actions on our behalf in the past – for the privilege of prayer itself. Take the disposition of joy. Keep your nose up. Refuse to fixate on the unmet need or obsess in worry. Wear grace as a garment. Refuse to be so self-absorbed that you cannot relate to others with a need in a caring way. Manage the weight of the problem with peace as your demeanor. It is an extraordinary standard, coupled with an exceptional privilege.

The Church in various ages has dismissed the need to verbalize their needs and concerns in prayer. The mystics would not mention their needs, they would only intone, *"Thy will be done!"* As noble as such actions may appear, they are not God's way. He wants us to bring our needs to Him, to labor in explaining our needs and how He factors into those needs, as if we were informing Him for the first time, as if he had no knowledge of the problem. And then, we are to leave the need in His hands and wait for the answer. In such moments, our Father teaches us. He mentors us. He molds our values. He clarifies his purposes for our lives. Scriptures come alive. The Spirit sustains us. The joy of the Spirit and the peace of God are imparted.

Pray First Yourself. It is so important to go to the Lord first with your need, privately. Take the necessary time to lay out the problem. Search the Scripture and find a prayer platform. Wait on the Spirit.

Put the full weight of your confidence in Him. God wants you to learn to hear His voice for yourself. He wants you to discover the joy of personal breakthrough in prayer. This should be your practice, whenever possible, before you go public with the need.

Louis Pasteur believed, "Chance favors the prepared mind." Arm yourself with Scripture. Meditate on the passages that relate to your situation. Life is the laboratory in which God grows and develops us. He does not extricate us from every challenge. He will not give us a ride over every mountain. He wants us to be strong. Far too often, prayer requests are perceived by us as the means to escape pain and problems. It is precisely in the storm that God wishes us to experience peace. He longs to see us triumph over the trouble. To learn, *"Greater is He that is in me…"* Pray first, for yourself.

Engage Friends to Pray. There are some things that overwhelm us. When you cannot pray effectively for yourself, you cannot think clearly or bear the pain - others must pray for you. When Israel was in a battle with Amalek, Moses was on the mountain praying as they fought. As long as the hands of Moses were raised in prayer, Israel prevailed (Exodus 17:11). What a difference intercession can make. After a season in this painful posture, Moses could no longer continue to lift his hands, and Israel began to taste defeat. Here God gives a picture revealing the direct connection between the intercession of Moses and the tide of the battle. Imagine – your prayer for another can turn the tide of their battle. This is not merely a mystical thing. It is practical, measurable, real and palpable.

Finally, Aaron and Hur stood beside Moses and lifted his hands for him and sat him on a rock. Here is prayer for the pray-*er*. Intercession for the intercessor. There are times when a person, a pastor, a Mayor, a leader, is critical to some outcome, but they are too weary to effectively function. Others must pray for them or the battle will be lost. At times, the warfare is exhausting. All we can do is be seated on the rock, Christ, and allow others to lift our hands and pray for us, and the battle turns.

While Wesley Duewel was in India, he had barely missed one anti-Christian riot, and found himself in the middle of another angry, unruly mob. They began to shout at him, but somehow he passed through their midst without even being touched. He would learn later, that at home, an intercessor was praying for his protection at that very hour, though the prayer warrior had no specific knowledge of the circumstances.[10] O the power of intercession! O the privilege of prayer requests.

Find a Prayer Partner. A prayer partner can be a lifesaver. Having someone you can call and *ask to pray for you* is next to heaven. Having someone that *you pray with,* often, regularly – is heaven, at least on earth. As you pray with someone, look for compatibility. Look for a hot heart. Look for someone nearby for face-to-face praying. Look for someone of the same gender. Look for someone with understanding. Look for permanence – a long-term relationship. Develop a plan. Consider parameters – what are the limits of contact? How much can you, should you share? Keep it mutual. Keep it confidential. Keep the relationship growing.

Join a Small Prayer Group. *"I thank my God upon every remembrance of you"* (Philippians 1:3; 2 Timothy 1:3). Imagine someone saying to you, 'Every time I think about you, I offer prayerful thanks to God.' That is Paul's intercessory posture toward the church at Philippi, and his friend Timothy. There is power in our agreement in prayer. Someone said, "A men's accountability group meeting in Jesus' name has more spiritual power than the Joint Chiefs of Staff have military power. A family Bible study has more authority than a meeting of the U. S. Supreme Court."[11] Sometimes a prayer partnership will evolve into a small prayer group. At other times, small prayer groups are intentionally formed.

Explore. Check your church bulletin to see if there are small prayer groups already functioning that are "open" to others. Some groups are closed – they are covenant prayer groups focused on a cause; they are maxed out in terms of size (five to 12 is the ideal size). Find someone on the inside of an open group and try it out.

Determine. Make sure you know what kind of group you are looking for. Prayer groups have different functions. Some are *prayer support groups* that essentially focus on the needs of one another, sharing prayer requests. Others focus on some mission cause (near or far), with personal prayer needs considered, but on a back burner. Some prayer groups are homogeneous – mothers, dads, men, women, single moms, former addicts, couples, divorced, etc. With whom and about what do you want to pray?

Listen. When it's prayer time at your church, listen to the music of prayer. Listen for the voice that seems to rise to a different level in prayer – not volume, but spirit. Are they in a prayer group? Do they lead one? You catch prayer. You want to be around people of prayer. Listen. You'll hear them. You feel safe praying with them. They encourage and motivate, and you are built up in your faith because of their prayer pattern.

Desire. Tell God your desire to be part of a small mutual, peer-type prayer group. Allow the Holy Spirit to cultivate that desire deep within you. Be dependent on Him. Let Him lead. This is not a head thing; it is a heart thing.

Follow. Follow the Holy Spirit's guidance. That may mean following someone with a hot-heart to their prayer meeting. Or, it may mean asking them to come as a guest and help you start a prayer group, serving as a mentor. Invite others to come and explore the possibility of beginning a prayer group together. Ask for only the one time commitment. Look at it like a date. If you have a dozen, and you actually end up with half returning, you have done well. Explore a foundational partnership – the next four-to-six week, then a more permanent commitment beyond that. Remember, prayer groups typically have their greatest season of effectiveness in the sixth-to-eighteenth months after the group has jelled a bit, but before it becomes too comfortable and complacent – a "cliquish inside" group.

Once your group is in the formative stage, establish some guidelines.

1. **Agree on the Format.** What are the components? The greatest threat to vertical prayer is horizontal sharing. That is, we talk rather than pray. Agree on a schedule. Five minutes – settle in. Pray for the central focus on the group. Pray for immediate needs. Wait on God. Share Scripture impressions. End at a certain time.

2. **Agree on the Group Membership.** Is the group open? Can anyone come? Who is committed?

3. **Agree to Attend.** Once you establish membership, remember the cause to which you have committed to pray, the cause or missionary that you are praying for, etc. deserves faithfulness.

4. **Agree to Engage.** Participate. Pray.

5. **Agree to Disengage.** Turn off cell-phones. They invite intrusion and distraction.

6. **Agree to be Expeditious.** Begin on time and end of time. Focus on the prayer cause around which the group is organized. Refuse to let personal needs press out the organizing cause.

7. **Agree to Keep Agreeing.** Do a quarterly check. Are you still on the same page? If not, redraw your prayer group focus. Or consider blessing others to create another group focused on another need.

8. **Agree with and acknowledge God.** Make God the center figure – not needs, not people, not problems.

9. **Agree to Be Personal.** Keep things warm and cordial.

10. **Agree on the Focus.** Every group needs to organized around something bigger than personal needs.

11. **Agree to Stay Focused.** Stay focused on the organizing need – missions, a nation, a cause, etc.

12. **Agree to Be There and Leave Things There.** Be committed. Make attendance a priority. And whatever is shared of a personal nature – leave there.

Pray Together as a Couple

According to George Barna, 23 percent of non-Christians experience divorce. Among born-again Christians, the number recently was 27 percent. Among "Fundamentalist Christians," 30 percent have experienced a divorce. *FamilyLife* ° from its extensive research found that less than eight percent of Christian couples pray together on a regular basis. That is shockingly low. When Christian couples do actively pray together, the divorce rate is less than one percent. True to the aphorism, "Couples who pray together, stay together." No other action comes close in terms of securing the relationship. African American couples are more likely to share core religious beliefs and pray together (40 percent) at home than Anglo or Hispanic couples (29 percent).[12] Praying together leads to a shared spiritual identity as a couple. A surprising discovery was made that the ethnic gulf narrowed along key factors manifesting more homogeneity. "What this study suggests is that religion is one of the key factors narrowing the racial divide in relationship quality in the United States," researchers said. The strongest difference-maker was praying or reading the Bible together.

When a husband and wife go to God as a couple, heaven keeps a record and notices the humble act of divine dependence. Unified prayer intensifies the importance and the value of praying. When a wife hears her husband humbling himself before God, it increases her sense of safety and ratchets up her trust level. Each partner reveals their deepest concerns in prayer. Humility draws God into the equation. He exalts the humble. The open channel of vertical communication with God amplifies the horizontal. It nurtures intimacy. Couples start hearing one another more clearly. God is openly and declaratively invited into the marriage – its problems and the possibilities. As sin and shortcomings are confessed, grace abounds. Love flourishes. Honesty is the foundation for a healthy marriage, and the presence of God is the safest place for bedrock honesty to take place.

Prayer demonstrates commitment to God – together. It recertifies the marriage and the home as belonging to God's Kingdom, marking it spiritually. Jude declared prayer to be the means by which *"we build ourselves up on our most holy faith."* Marriages are built up in the same way, and yet 92 percent of Christian couples do not pray together. We may have identified the greatest weakness in the Christian home, and therefore the church and the whole community, religious and secular.

Here are some tips for beginning to pray together as a couple:

1. Establish a mutually good time.
2. Start out with a short prayer time.
3. Be real. Don't try to be spiritual.
4. Let your prayer time grow.
5. Pray "bite-sized" prayers.
6. Don't pray selfish prayers.
7. Be authentic.
8. Don't fear a stretch of silence.
9. Watch for the Spirit.
10. Pray for your marriage.

One couple noted, "Praying together as a couple is something that is very intimate…it adds another level of closeness." Couples say that in times of disagreement, when one can't see the other's point of view, one will say: "Let's pray." Inviting God to be the arbitrator is a slice of genius. "Prayer is the great reconciler," couples confess. And in a fast-paced, dizzying world, prayer is the speed-bump that slows things down and keeps the marriage grounded. It is the moment to connect, to act out the belief that "this too will pass" and confirm eternal values. Every decision is an opportunity to invite God into a partnership. No matter is too inconsequential for prayer.

Pray Together as a Family for Needs

A lady called a cab, and when it arrived, she brought three small children out, and put them all in the back-seat. "Start the meter," she ordered, "I'll be right back." But she wasn't. As the driver waited, the small children moved beyond restlessness to nerve-racking noise. They bawled and yelled. The driver was beside himself – a hostage to the little tyrants. After about 15 minutes, the mother returned and opened the door, retrieving all three children. "How much do I owe you?" she enquired. The driver was incredulous, "You called a cab – aren't you going somewhere?" She shook her head, "No. I just needed a few minutes of peace and quiet. Here's the fare. Thanks for waiting. I may call you tomorrow." One of the great stress relievers for at-home Moms is a husband and father who understands her need to escape to a grown-up world after hours and days in isolation. The simple power of shared prayer, of support, of space for private time is critical to both mental and spiritual health.

Prayer Requests at Church

In so many churches, the way in which we handle prayer requests is tired – boring and ineffective. One denominational leader was in a different church each Sunday over a six-month period. He kept a running total of the time it took to "share" prayer requests and the actual time "prayed." According to his unofficial tallies, the average time dedicated to the litany of woes on Sunday morning averaged between eight and nine minutes. The amount of prayer never exceeded 90 seconds.

Find creative ways to give place to prayer requests, but in a new and more meaningful way. Have people offer their needs as written prayer requests placed in the offering baskets. Hold them up before God. Then place the prayer request cards in the prayer room. Have staff follow-up on them. Have elders or prayer leaders form a line and pray for needs during a portion of the praise and worship time. Engage the congregation in prayer. Make the sanctuary more than a meeting room – make it a prayer room, one that is respected seven days a week. Start prayer groups who meet at the church for prayer regularly. Open the altars for extended seasons of seeking God, after the formal service has ended. Engage intercessors in praying for needs. Offer prayer for healing and other needs. Do small groups of prayer during your worship time or in the altar service. Make sure the staff is meeting together to pray.

The Prayer Needs of the Community

If we use the privilege of prayer requests only for ourselves, for insiders, as "member benefits," we will miss a great opportunity for evangelism. The world around us, including family and friends, is full of needs. And many want so much to touch God. Surprisingly, they are very open to prayer. Some churches put up "Prayer Stations." They rent a spot at the local flea market or county fair and offer to give the gift of prayer. The rewards for the intercessors involved is priceless. The impact may be eternal. Other churches encourage members to place "prayer request boxes" at different locations where they shop or dine. The prayer boxes allow anyone to write down a need. The requests are harvested at least once a week. Some are anonymous. Some are complete with contact information. Some are general. Some are quite personal and poignant. It is obvious, people are hungry for prayer. As Christians pray for others, especially for non-believers, they open a door for God to reveal Himself to hurting people. It is a natural doorway to evangelism. Shouldn't the church be a place that cares and prays for the community, and not just for itself?

Living Outside Your Circle of Pain

Howard Rees was "cynical, bitter and resentful of life." Rees described himself as "a burden" both to himself and others.

> I was crippled at two-and-a-half years of age and resented the raw deal that life had given me. Then I met a girl who changed my entire life. She had what I lacked, a quiet, inner poise, a warmth and friendship, an irresistible power of helping others merely by her presence. Finally, I asked her what it was. She simply said, 'I have something to live for. I have given my life completely, with no reservations, one hundred per cent to the Christ, and now through Him I'm living for others. Before that time my life was like a merry-go-round; I went around in circles getting nowhere.'

Rees said the story changed his life. "I gave up indulging in self-pity; in fact, I forgot myself in helping others, and now I, too, know what she had, for I have it also, and there is nothing like it in all life's experiences."[13] It has been observed,

> Resentment is a form of hurt ego. It is an outgrowth of self-pity – a rebellion against events or people who have thrust at one's pride, interests, ambitions. One who is given to resentment feels he has been frustrated by an act or event. The way to overcome resentment is to step outside of self.[14]

Paul modeled this kind of living while he was at Philippi. Many of us have never seen anyone else live this way. *"What you learned"* – it was taught. What you *"received"* – perceptually got your head around. Concepts you cognitively and behaviorally *"owned."*

What you *"heard and saw"* – Paul lived out these principles in word and deed. The believers at Philippi had seen them in action. Now, they were to *"do"* them – to act them out. They were to behave differently than the world around them since they now had the privilege of prayer. Their thinking and acting had changed. Lily Tomlin once said, "I always wanted to be somebody, but I should have been more specific."

The story is told of a little girl, orphaned and confused, hurt and angry, and finally, uncontrollable and institutionalized. One day, peering through the bars at the window, she realized that she had imprisoned herself, that the iron bars were not the most constraining thing in her life. She had allowed life to dictate her emotions and limit her choices. She had always reacted, rather than being pro-active. She scribbled a note and pressed it through the narrow space at the edge of the window, "Whoever finds this note, I love you!" She watched the wind pick up the piece of paper and carry it away and somehow she saw herself as free, no longer confined. Her change in thinking, altered her perspective of the world. The ownership of her destiny was found in the choice to act and not react. It liberated her and started her down a path of healing.

REVIEW It

1. *If you ask in My name, I will* _____.
2. God takes the route that brings Him the most _____.
3. Our attitude should not change, but the _____ to a problem is dynamic.
4. First, pray for _____. Then share the need with others.
5. We serve a God who _____.

TALK About It

1. Discuss the idea of the New Testament as a "will" – the estate of Christ. Do you understand that concept?

2. The mystics would not mention their needs. Do you resist being vulnerable enough to share a prayer need?

3. How do we hold up one another's arms in a way that brings victory, not only for them, but for us as well? What does that say to the connection between needs and relationships?

4. In the "Great Exchange" – emphasize what are we trading? When making a prayer request, there are certain things we should know that will strengthen our prayer life. What are they?

5. If we pray for ourselves in faith, why would we then ask others to pray for us – would that not be an indication of faithlessness? How do we balance personal faith, and the need at times to 'borrow faith' from others? Emphasize and gauge our legalism.

Endnotes

1. Public Domain, 1905.
2. J. Sarno, *The Mind-Body Prescription* (New York: Warner, 1998).
3. Don Colbert, *Deadly Emotions: Understanding the Mind-Body-Spirit Connection That Can Heal or Destroy You* (Nashville: Thomas Nelson; 2003), 58.
4. Michael Hart, *The 100: A Ranking of the Most Influential Persons in History* (New York: A Citadel Press Book, Carrol Publishing, 1993), 188.
5. David Foster, *Accept No Mediocre Life: Living Beyond Labels, Libels, and Limitations* (Faithwords, 2007), 48.
6. Morgan, *More Stories,* 161-162.
7. Colbert, 21.
8. Ibid, 205.
9. Bruce Larson, *The Presence: Finding God When You've Lost Your Way* (Harper: San Francisco, 1990), 126.
10. Wesley Duewel, *Touch the World Through Prayer* (Zondervan, 1986), 27.
11. Will Davis, Jr. *Pray Big* (Grand Rapids: MI; Revell, 2007), 102.

12. Donna St. George, *Journal of Marriage and Family* (Thursday, August 12, 2010). Co-author, W. Bradford Wilcox, Director of the National Marriage Project at the University of Virginia.

13. www.washingtonpost.com/wp-dyn/content/article/2010/08/11/AR2010081101961.html.

14. Ibid, 56-57.

REVIEW It Answers

1. Do it
2. Glory
3. Approach
4. Yourself
5. Acts

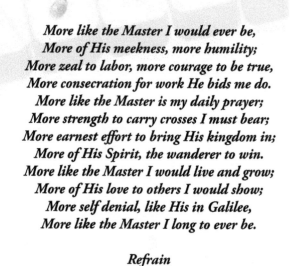

More like the Master I would ever be,
More of His meekness, more humility;
More zeal to labor, more courage to be true,
More consecration for work He bids me do.
More like the Master is my daily prayer;
More strength to carry crosses I must bear;
More earnest effort to bring His kingdom in;
More of His Spirit, the wanderer to win.
More like the Master I would live and grow;
More of His love to others I would show;
More self denial, like His in Galilee,
More like the Master I long to ever be.

Refrain
Take Thou my heart, I would be Thine alone;
Take Thou my heart, and make it all Thine own.
Purge me from sin, O Lord, I now implore,
Wash me and keep me Thine forevermore.[1]

CHAPTER TWELVE
Step Ten: Certify the Jurors

Whatever things are true, whatever things are noble, whatever things are just, whatever things are pure, whatever things are lovely, whatever things are of good report, if there is any virtue and if there is anything praiseworthy – meditate on these things.

Perspective: The problem is not the enemy without, but the traitors within. The trouble that assails, the crisis that puzzles, the dilemma for which there seems no solution, the danger that promises certain peril – none of these are as potentially deadly as the enemy within. Jesus was a conqueror, not by changing the external circumstances, but by retaining inner peace as the sentry of His soul. The guard of His castle was never overrun. He never tumbled. He never lost his footing. The mind is the battlefield of the soul. Having the mind of Christ is the key both to peace and power. What does the mind of Christ look like? How do we measure it, describe it? Paul gives us a profile of eight traits that characterize Christ-like thinking. If our decisions resonate with these nine exemplar values, we will always find ourselves in perfect peace.

P sychologist Ruth Brenda did an experiment with teens. Placing them in groups of ten, each was instructed to raise a hand when the teacher pointed to the longest line of three lines displayed on three separate charts. The test was rigged. One person in each group was not told that the nine others had been instructed to always vote for the second longest line. When hands went up for the obviously wrong answer, the tenth student appeared confused, disoriented, and then inevitably lifted a conforming hand. Peer pressure, group conformity, subtle but still compelling, won out 75 percent of the time. Younger students were equally vulnerable.[2] Abraham Lincoln declared, "I desire so to conduct the affairs of this administration that if, at the end, when I come to lay down the reins of power, I have lost every other friend on earth, I shall at least have one friend left, and that friend shall be down inside of me."[3] The courage to stand all alone is indispensable in a worldly age. Even Nietzsche believed, "The most common lie is the lie one tells to oneself."[4] As someone cryptically observed, "Forbidden fruits make bad jams."

Key Principle

The problem is not only the enemy without, but the traitors within. The mind is the battlefield of the soul. Paul gives us a profile of eight traits that characterize Christ-like thinking. If our decisions resonate with these exemplar values, we will find ourselves with inner peace, with joy – poise.

The Perfect Jury

When we are pressed with needs, our mind is where the battle is fought between faith and doubt; between raising up God-like ideas and pulling down unbiblical notions. If we win the battle here, we win the battle finally and certainly. Paul placed this section *after* his discussion on prayer requests, but this is integral to the whole idea.

Let's proceed with a kind of allegory. Envision your mind as a kind of courtroom where you make life decisions. Evidence is presented by your senses – objective facts about which you are required to make judgments and determine a course of action. As Christians, we are to decide and act in ways that glorify Christ. Every decision and action is to be submitted to the Lordship of Christ. Every decision is to be made in the light of Scripture.

The Jurors. Here we meet what we might call the Inner Court of our Soul (or mind). Paul names eight influencers – Mr. True, Mr. Noble, Mr. Just, Mr. Pure, Mr. Lovely, Mr. Good Report, along with Mr. Virtue and Mr. Praiseworthy. By these filters, we are to weigh decisions. If we possessed the discipline to process all our thoughts, our words and deeds, in light of these eight values, we would make decisions that honored Christ. Remember, by the nature of spiritual warfare, we win or lose battles by healthy or flawed thinking patterns. Let's investigate, by the use of this analogy, how those mental battles are won or lost.

Make the Decision to Act. Paul urges *"The things which you have learned and received"* – do them. He taught the principles and supposedly, they 'learned' them. His concern is that they might not have 'received' or grasp them. Had they only *heard the words* or had they *owned the concept?* Was the principle only in their heads or also in their hearts? Were they still considering the teaching? Or were they acting, living the ideas? The difference is between *perceiving* truth and practicing truth, not merely *hearing words.* Between conceptual understanding – and applying it to life. The Biblical notion is always "hearing *unto obedience."* It is hearing that moves one to act. If someone yells, "Fire, fire, fire!" and you believe the words, you won't sit still.

Increasingly, science is uncovering the connection between the mind and the body, and the findings are astounding. In every cell of your body are *neuropeptides* – called *thinking cells.* The neuropeptides are chains of amino acids that travel through the circuitry of the nervous system. They are like keys that open the molecular locks in every cell of the body, interfacing with a specific class of immune cells, the *monocytes.*[5] These special agents of the mind with their high security clearance are scattered throughout the body. Researchers call them little "bits of brain" moving through the body. By them, the brain *talks* to the immune cells all over the body. The neuropeptides also convey information back to the brain. When the brain registers fear, hurt or frustration, every cell in the body is alerted and very quickly.[6] These cells have a kind of memory! Our reactions then are not only mental – they are cellular! Fear alone triggers 1,400 known physical and chemical stress reactions. It activates more than 30 different hormones and neurotransmitters.[7] To override these habitual responses requires a great deal of mental discipline. The effort is worth it, since chronic stress puts nearly every organ in the body at risk.[8]

Make the Bible the Basis of the Decision. Courts are institutions of law. Judges and juries rule on the basis of a fixed, rational, and objective standard. Our pleas to heaven, our prayers, are also based on rational, objective truth, on God's law, on incontrovertible spiritual, social and moral principles. We are to live and make decisions within the bounds of these living principles, in consultation with Christ, the Lord of our lives, and that is called prayer! To pray inconsistently with Scripture is misguided, even defiant. We should pray about everything. In doing so, we submit every need, every choice, and every decision with a *"Not my will, but Your will be done"* disposition. Prayer is consultation with Christ over an open Bible. This is the way Christians are to live.

Monitor Your Mental Process. So Paul urges us to think as we pray. Prayer is not a mindless thing. *"Think on these things"* implies a logical and systematic analysis of the situation. In other places, the same Greek word is translated *account, reckon, reason* or *conclude!*

This is not casual thought, but serious reflection.[9] In the previous verses, Paul talked about prayer needs, focusing on our *actions* in the middle of a needy state. Now, he focuses on our *thinking*. He probes beyond and behind the need, under it.

Christians should *think*. They are not to feel their way through life's problems but to think when they pray. Intuitive discernment is wonderful – God does give His children a "word of wisdom or knowledge," but such moments must not displace a disciplined and transformed mind. We are to rationally weigh our choices, thinking about them as God thinks about them. This is not an easy or automatic thing. It requires a regiment of

> ...careful, disciplined meditation and contemplation to even begin to grasp the immensity of the truth God has for us. Therefore, a thoughtless Christian devoid of meditation and contemplation is a strange contradiction. He believes that he is heir to eternal truth which paradoxically he doesn't consider worth thinking about too seriously.[10]

Edward R. Murrow, the great news correspondent in the early days of network television, once said, "...a great many people think they are thinking when they are only rearranging their prejudices and superstitions." The Bible is our basis for reason. Through its lens, we gain a fresh new worldview. Each member of this inner Court of the Soul represents some aspect of our reasoning process.

Prayer – and the Mental Courtroom

Every person, whose fate has hung on the decision of a panel of jurors, has probably searched their faces during the trial. Is there kindness and understanding in their eyes? Are they alert? How do they react to the evidence, particularly evidence in your favor or decidedly against you? Did they catch that technicality? Will they obey the judge and ignore that biased statement?

Discern Mock Jurors. Think of your mind as a courtroom where evidence is presented and decisions are made which determine the outcomes in your life. Think of the jurors as these eight traits – true and noble, just and pure, lovely and of good report, virtue and praiseworthy. What if the qualified jurors had been supplanted by seditious substitutes who were actually plotting your destruction? What if, as you searched the faces of jurors in the course of the trial, you noted that Mr. Just, the qualified juror, who you trusted to rule appropriately, was gone? Instead, Mr. Unjust – unnoticed, undetected was sitting in his seat, wearing his robes pretentiously. What had happened to Mr. Just? Your eyes continue to survey other members of the jury. "Amazing," you say to yourself! Sitting in the place of Mr. Noble, wearing his robe, was Mr. Ignoble, also known as Mr. Frivolous. And in the place of Mr. Good Report was Mr. Critical, a personal enemy you knew all too well. Not all the jurors had been supplanted, but there were enough substitutes that you now feared the outcome. Decisions coming from this jury were likely to be dangerous verdicts. "Stop!" you want to shout. You want to interrupt the proceedings. "The jury has been rigged!" A godly decision can only be assured, if these surrogates are identified and disqualified, and the rightful jurors are reinstated.

Disqualify Unbiblical Ideas. We must "pull down imaginations" – these spurious and fleshly thinking patterns. We must demand that each inner juror be Biblically qualified. We must replace worldly thinking with godly thoughts, and earthly thinking with heavenly thinking, fleshly actions with Biblical actions. The root of the word *imaginations* is *image* – a reference to *idols*. Idolatry is not a matter of worshipping a mere material image, be it of gold or silver, wood or stone. It is allowing the thinking patterns, mental *images* represented by some pagan value system, to affect our world view. Satan does not need to possess us. He only needs to unduly influence our thinking patterns. If he can substitute untruth for truth, discord for loveliness and so on, he continues his hold on our lives. This battle is not in an external courtroom but in our minds. As long as we allow pseudo jurors to be seated as inner decision makers, we will make wrong assessments, allow unbiblical judgments, and make unchristian and deadly decisions.

Practice the Lord's Presence. We have the peace of God because the God of peace is with us. And we have an awareness of His presence – "the Lord is near" – because we have not allowed our peace, the sentry of our heart and mind, to be taken hostage. That is possible because we have employed a filtering process that decontaminates our thinking. It cleanses. It sanitizes. It disinfects the negative and impure thoughts, the skewed and polluting ideas. The result is that we live in a state of joy and grace. The witness we have is extraordinary. Joy, grace, peace, thanksgiving, effective prayer, answers from God, an undisturbed heart, a balanced and calm mind. All from prayer - prayer bathed in a perspective of gratitude. Prayer that is from a filtered mind.

Whatever you *received*, Paul urged, *do* habitually. Make it a consistent practice. If peace in the middle of a storm is possible, why do we lose it so often? The problem is not the tempest outside but the traitors within. We snuff out joy and gentleness by defective thinking patterns.

The Jurors of the Inner Court: A Proper Introduction

The Jurors – A Profile. Let's meet the members of the inner Supreme Court. They are:

NAME	MEANING	NOT
Mr. True	Genuine, authentic, real.	Not phony
Mr. Noble	Serious, sober.	Not frivolous, light, insincere.

Mr. Just	Right, righteous, fair, weighted.	Not wrong, corrupt, not legal, convenient.
Mr. Pure	Clean, holy, pristine.	Not dirty or filthy, Uncontaminated, Not soiled or used.
Mr. Lovely	Attractive, appealing.	Not repulsive, having beauty, being loving. Not discordant, dissident.
Mr. Good	Helpful, edifying, enlightening. Positive report.	Not hurtful, critical.
Mr. Virtue	Excellence, quality, the "best." First-class.	Not inferior or "left-over." Not second rate or damaged.
Mr. Praiseworthy	Positive	Not negative, not deserving the status of a model. Embarrassing. Not easily condemned or censured.[11]

Seating a Good Jury.

Let's look at each of these jurors in depth.

True – true in the sense of being *real, not phony*. Christianity demands real people, not phonies. Our God is real. Christ was real. Authenticity is demanded.[12] This is "truth-speaking" and "truth-being."[13] No fraud is permitted. No duplicity is allowed.

Honest – best understood as *noble or serious*.[14] It is the idea of being honorable or venerable. This is behavior that garners respect, esteem, and the admiration of others.[15] This is *serious* as contrasted with *frivolous*. It is carrying oneself in a way that displays self-respect. We know that Christians are to be joyous, so this is not a heavy or brooding personality that makes us appear ghastly and unpleasant.

But our faith demands a depth that dignifies.[16] Honest is also the notion of being honorable or revered. It is behavior that invites reverence. A venerable one.[17] It is an appreciation for things that produce a noble seriousness.[18]

Just – the idea of *right as opposed to convenient.* This is the willingness to move outside our comfort zone to stand for what is right. We will not retreat quietly into the shadows. We are people of conscience whose sense of right and wrong, of justice and righteousness has now been acutely sharpened because of the mind of Christ. Joseph of Arimathea was a "just man" who was moved to think in just ways and, therefore, to act out those ways.[19]

Jesus was buried in his tomb. Pilate was not a just man. In his struggle with right and wrong, he had sought to absolve himself of the guilt of wrong doing by washing his hands of Christ. He wanted distance between himself and Jesus. Joseph not only identified with Jesus, he did the risky thing! Only the body of a family member was placed in a man's tomb. Joseph included Jesus in his family! He made this choice, and as far as he knew, Jesus was permanently dead! There was no value to be seen by such a dangerous association. How could He be the Messiah? He was dead. There was nothing to be gained by Joseph's action except the possible disdain of family and friends, the ire of Jewish authorities, and the potential dishonor some would say he had brought to his own family burial vault. The image of Pilate's pitiful cowardice will live in infamy. And as long as men are on the earth, they will journey to Joseph's empty family tomb and stand in wonder. Just men act in righteous and bold ways in moment's of crisis. Such acts come to define us and our families forever. Just means righteous. And righteous men do just things.

Pure – *clean, as opposed to dirty.*[20] This is a call for "a holy chastity of thought and act."[21] Pure is purity in all things.

Lovely – the idea of *relating in a way that promotes brotherly love.*

It is being loving as opposed to being discordant.[22] The believer is to be a "peacemaker." He is to be amiable and pleasing.[23] He builds bridges and not barriers.[24] Lovely is the thing which itself excites love and makes the one who says or does certain things endearing to others – winsome, pleasing, amiable.[25]

Good report – being *helpful, and not critical.* Chronic negativism is not the mark of the faith-filled Christian.[26] It may be the idea of being "sweet spoken"[27] instead of bitter. Of speaking in a kind and winning way. Of good report is the notion of "sounding well." Speaking in a winning and gracious way, an attractive[28] rather than repelling or offensive way.[29]

Virtue – not our idea of virtue or character, but the *notion of excellence!* [30] Excellence as opposed to inferior. The Old Testament condemned crippled animals as sacrifices. Malachi called them an abomination. We do not offer to God our leftovers. Second best is not good enough for Him. Virtue is the Hebrew notion of praise. It conveys moral excellence.[31]

"If there be any praise" – think on those things! *Dwell on the positive, what's right,* and not what is wrong. What is worthy of praise? This is an admonition to positive thinking. It is a call to see the bright side and not only the dark side. You think positively and not negatively. You see possibilities and not merely the impossible. "Caleb and Joshua came back with grapes – the rest with gripes."[32]

These standards provide a filter or thinking process that serves as an assistant to effective praying. Using the analogy of the court, Jesus, the inner Chief Justice, is in perfect agreement with all eight of His legitimate juror partners. These are all, in truth, extensions of His character. The goal in prayer is to get a unanimous decision with all eight jurors in agreement. If you pray about something and one or more of the members of the court are in disagreement, it should be a red flag. To ask the heavenly court to do something that is a violation of the character of God is not only war against heaven, it is war against the self. It divides the mind.

He was only eight years old when his father announced to him that he would have to buy his own clothes. So the young lad ran errands, collected and sold junk. He even invested in a pig to raise and sell. Soon he had purchased a dozen pigs, but with complaints rising from neighbors his father curbed his ambitious enterprise, "We can't take advantage of our neighbors." The kid would remember the value of balancing enterprise with the rights of neighbors in mind, of fair and decent treatment for the rest of his life. As an adult, his first venture, a butcher shop failed, because he would not supply a free bottle of bourbon to the chef of the local hotel.

In Kemmerer, Wyoming, he opened "The Golden Rule Store." Within two years, he had expanded to three stores and instituted profit sharing for his employees. By 1912, he owned 34 stores, enough to motivate him to move his headquarters to New York City. At the age of 39, he retired and became Chairman of the Board. By 1924, his personal income was more than $1.5 billion annually. Much of that, he gave to charitable and Christian causes.[33] In 1929, he had 1,400 stores across the nation, a formidable retail chain, all driven by pure values. The code of ethics was "a fair remuneration and not all the profit the traffic will bear." He believed in giving back.

The company tested every policy, method and act by this question, "Does it square with what is right and just?" When the Great Depression came, it nearly wiped him out. In 1910, he had lost his first wife. In 1923, his second wife died in childbirth. When the stock market drop came, his company stock plummeted from 120 dollars a share to 13. He was virtually broke. He recalled an overwhelming temptation, a "darkness that had settled upon me." He wanted to drown his sorrows.

At times, he walked the streets and prayed, battling his depression and deadly desires. He checked into a sanitarium, fought his way back to health, regained faith and vitality, and started the long climb back to financial dominance. In 1951, he had a store in every state and his sales passed the $1 billion mark. Even when peers mocked what they considered old-fashioned values, he stuck to his guns. For a season, he wrote a column for the *Christian Herald* magazine. His name was James Cash (J. C.) Penney.[34]

The stages of Decision Making

TRUE: First, separate *untruths* from *truth*, the real from the *phony*. Allow no *insincere* thing to proceed. Permit no *hypocrisy*, no inner duplicity. If it is not true, if it requires that you be less than true and authentic, don't move forward. Resist that thought. Lock that door. Don't let that idea rise up.

NOBLE: Ask the second question. Is it noble? Is it frivolous and less than serious? Is it light and compromising in some crude way? Will it promote dignity and graciousness, poise and saintliness? Is it the kind of thing that would be done by a holy man or woman of God? If not, say "No."

JUST: Now the third question. Is it also just or right and righteous? Is it godly? Is it the right thing, the right decision, even if it is costly? Or is the convenient thing to do? Choose right, even if it is costly.

PURE: Then the fourth question. Is it pure? Is it clean or is it dirty in a lewd or compromising way? Does it offend holiness? Is it degrading?

LOVELY: Is it lovely? Is it the kind of thing that promotes you, and therefore Christ, as being loving and lovable? Is it the kind of thing that makes you less than lovable? Does it put up some kind of barrier? Does it contribute to discord or accord? Is it ugly – in action or character? Don't do it. Don't say it. Don't wear it. Don't watch it.

GOOD REPORT: Is it admirable, that is, of good report? Is it helpful and not merely critical?

VIRTUOUS: Does it promote excellence? Is it a crippled sacrifice, less than the best, your leftovers offered to God? Is it inferior or exceptional? Does it foster admiration or disdain? Offer God your brightest and best.

PRAISEWORTHY: Is it praiseworthy? Is it positive and not negative? Is it worthy of commendation and tribute? Is it the kind of action that will win acclaim and honor? Is it either the words or deed that others, deep inside, will recognize as admirable and worthy of emulation?

Imagine these eight values as inner tenants of the mind, guardians of godly thinking. If you own an apartment building and you rent out space to criminals, to gangsters and alcoholics, to addicts and deadbeats, you will soon have a major crisis. They will not only destroy their private space, but they will pollute common areas as well. The entire complex will soon reflect their undisciplined values. Other tenants will flee. Disorder will replace any sense of order and predictability. In the same way, if you rent out too much space in your mind for worry and fear, for depressing thoughts and distress, those hysterical and violent tenants, will take over your entire complex – your whole body.[35]

Value-based lives and organizations, like those of J. C. Penney above, seem to have gone by the wayside. Here is another profile, one of a completely different generation of leaders from our time, almost a century later. This representative and pace-setting group numbers more than 500. Considering their national influence and rank, their values should be stellar, impeccable, unimpeachable, unsullied. And yet, in a not too distant year, 84 members of this group were stopped for drunk driving and released after they claimed legal immunity.

They are beyond the law on this matter and in that jurisdiction.

This group of elites spend time in their private clubs or another one of a dozen DC watering holes. And they drive home drunk. Quite a picture! The DC police issued 2,912 parking tickets to cars owned by members of this group in one year. None were paid. They will haul away cars belonging to ordinary citizens, but they do not go after this group. What illustrious law-breaking group is this? The Congress of the United States.

One list details the criminal charges against 33 members of this group over the last two decades with plenty of wrong on both sides of the aisle.[36] The charges include tax evasion and perjury, obstruction of justice and extortion, racketeering and falsification of documents, theft and dealing in counterfeit merchandise, bribery and fraud, felony and forgery, spouse abuse, and physical assault. One was caught running a prostitution service from his home. These are our leaders!

Citizens for Responsibility and Ethics in Washington (CREW), a non-partisan activist group, found that 72 members of Congress diverted some $5.1 million in campaign funds to their relatives, or companies owned by their relatives over the past six years. The list includes 41 Republicans and 31 Democrats.[37] Scandals have persisted throughout American history, but they seem to be escalating. Twenty years ago the Keating Five precipitated the Savings and Loan crisis. Five senators were tainted with alleged kickbacks. The financial fix cost taxpayers $2 billion dollars. Yet, only reprimands were handed out, and that was the extent of the discipline.

In the same period, The House Bank was forced to temporarily close. Congressmen were abusing their accounts. The Government Accountability Office reported in one year, House members had written 8,331 bad checks. Even after reforms, 134 members wrote 4,325 bad checks, 581 of which were written for more than $1,000.[38] In 2005, the *San Diego Union-Tribune* reported a bribery scandal involving lobbyists' gifts and payments to a Representative, while the *Washington Post* reporters uncovered yet another congressional corruption involving fraud and bribery. The sexual misconduct is relentless with some 17 in the last two decades, not including the White House scandal or Presidential hopefuls.[39] What a mess!

"A people who values privileges above principles will soon lose both," declared President Dwight Eisenhower. "If we expect to travel with Jesus to a new heaven, we must prevail with Jesus for a new earth,"[40] and that requires reputable values. Such values begin with a renewed Christ-like mind. Not with a view of prayer that is always a request to escape the problem, but with a view that 'thinks' prayerfully over an open Bible. God wants integrity in our lives – the world is watching.

REVIEW It

1. The problem is not the enemy without, but the traitors

   _____.

2. Spiritual warfare is first an issue of the _____.

3. Imaginations represent thinking patterns, but there is a deeper connection with the terms images or idols. And that ties to the idea of our _____.

4. Paul urges us to _____ as we pray.

5. Prayer is consultation with Christ, over an open

   _____.

TALK About It

1. Talk about the idea of the mind as a kind of mental court where decisions are made.

2. List the jurors and talk about each character.

3. Which of these areas do you find is most difficult to maintain?

4. Talk about idolatry, not as a physical idol or icon, but as a conceptual world view.

5. Discuss the eight stages of decision making – the process of praying through life choices. Or, of getting a decision from a healthy inner jury.

Endnotes

1. Charles H. Gabriel, "More Like the Master" (Copyright: Public Domain; 1906).
2. David Foster, *Accept No Mediocre Life: Living Beyond Labels, Libels, and Limitations* (Faithwords, 2007), 106.
3. Quoted by David Foster, 31.
4. Ibid, 35.
5. Candace Pert, etc., "Opiate Agonists and Antagonists Discriminated by Receptor Binding in the Brain," (Science, 182; 1973), 1359-1361.
6. Paul Pearsall, *The Pleasure Prescription* (Alameda, CA; Hunter House Publishers, 1996), 90.
7. B. Hafen, K. Frandsen, K. Karen, etc., "The Health Effects of Attitudes, Emotions, and Relationships" (Provo, Utah; EMS Associates, 1992).
8. Don Colbert, *Deadly Emotions: Understand the Mind-Body-Spirit Connection That Can Heal Or Destroy You* (Nashville, TN: Thomas Nelson, 2006), 25-27.
9. Stuart Briscoe, *Bound for Joy: Philippians – Paul's Letter from Prison* (Regal: Glendale, CA, 1975), 144.
10. Ibid, 145.
11. Briscoe, 145f.
12. Briscoe, 145.
13. H. C. G. Moule. *Studies in Philippians* (Grand Rapids, MI: Kregel; 1977), 114.
14. Briscoe, 147.
15. Moule, 114.
16. Briscoe, 147.
17. M. R. Vincent. *Word Studies in the New Testament, Volume II* (MacDonald Publishing Company, MacDill Air Force Base, Tampa, FL), 892.
18. Kenneth Wuest. *Wuest's Word Studies, Philippians in the Greek New Testament* (Grand Rapids, MI: Eerdmans, 1942), 110.
19. Briscoe, 148.
20. Ibid, 149.
21. Moule, 114.

22. Briscoe, 150.
23. Moule, 114.
24. Briscoe, 150.
25. Wuest, 111.
26. Briscoe, 151.
27. Moule, 115.
28. Wuest, 111.
29. Vincent, 892.
30. Briscoe, 152.
31. Vincent, 892.
32. Briscoe, 152.
33. en.wikipedia.org/wiki/James_Cash_Penney.
34. www.prnewswire.com/news-releases/james-cash-penney-would-have-been-123-years-old-today-76613557.html
35. Colbert, 124.
36. www.wwco.com/~dda/criminals.php.
37. Doug Thompson, *Capitol Hill Blue News Service* (www.capitol-hillblue.com
38. Fox News Online, *Timeline: Congressional Scandals* (Sunday, January 15, 2006) www.foxnews.com/story/0,2933,181733,00.html.
39. List compiled by John Dean. writ.news.findlaw.com/dean/cong-sexscandals.html
40. Attributed to George King.

REVIEW It Answers
1. Within
2. Mind
3. Value/Belief System
4. Think
5. Bible

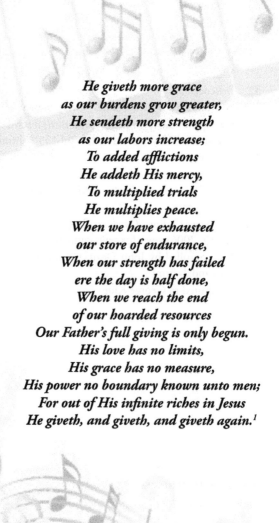

He giveth more grace
as our burdens grow greater,
He sendeth more strength
as our labors increase;
To added afflictions
He addeth His mercy,
To multiplied trials
He multiplies peace.
When we have exhausted
our store of endurance,
When our strength has failed
ere the day is half done,
When we reach the end
of our hoarded resources
Our Father's full giving is only begun.
His love has no limits,
His grace has no measure,
His power no boundary known unto men;
For out of His infinite riches in Jesus
He giveth, and giveth, and giveth again.[1]

Summary

The message of Paul is quite simple, and yet somewhat complex! It takes a bit of concentration to grasp the breadth of his challenge to the Philippian believers, and to us.

The essence of the passage is ultimately not about prayer requests or the pulsating felt needs that are ever with us. It is about our witness. The aggravations of this current world must not consume our emotions and cloud our thinking, affecting joy and peace. This was not theory to Paul. He had modeled this in the jailhouse in the city of Philippi itself.

1. Rejoice. That call to rejoice demands that we import the joy of heaven. It is more than an attitude change. It demands action. We rejoice. And we do so unconditionally. And this action aligns us with heaven's victory. Heaven knows no sorrow. It harbors no broken hearts. It encounters no set-backs. It suffers no wounds or want. Heaven knows only victory. Such extraordinary and indomitable victory is not known here. Our victories are intermittent, temporary, sometimes small and short-lived. There, victory is eternal. Such victory must be imported. "Rejoice!" Not in the standing and relief offered by this world, but "in the Lord!" And do so *always. Again, I say, Rejoice!*"

2. Stay in Peace. This stream of imported joy fuels the "peace of God" that resides in our hearts. The victory of Christ celebrated perpetually in heaven assures peace. The dominance of God over any matter makes contenders and challengers pale. All things are under His feet. Though we do not yet see all things under His feet, we have met the risen Christ, and are assured that He is returning.

3. Practice the Presence of God. Dr. Bob May will never know the impact he has had on my life. He was one of my Bible college professors. He was anything but typical. He was famous for "chasing rabbits" during his lectures, and some students seemed to triumph in luring him down some trail of thought that didn't seem germane to the class focus.

In retrospect, it was those side-bar journeys that most impacted me. One day he began to hold forth on "practicing the presence of God." He encouraged us to imagine Jesus riding with us. I had seen the 1950 movie with Jimmy Stewart, an award winning film, in which he had a relationship with a six-foot-three-and-a-half inch "pooka" named Harvey. No one else could see the huge rabbit – but he could. Everywhere he went, he went with Harvey. And he carried on a conversation, to the dismay of his family. In the end, so the story goes, the invisible friend proved to be real!

I began to "practice" the presence of Jesus – not Harvey, Jesus. No one could see Him or hear Him. But I wanted to go everywhere with Him. On some mornings, though, the neighbors may have thought me as bizarre as Elwood Dowd, the character played by Stewart. I opened the passenger door for Jesus. On my way to class, He and I talked. This was before the day of cell phones. It isn't uncommon now to see someone alone in a car talking away and gesturing, all by themselves.

One day, sitting at the corner of Shaw and Herndon Avenue, I was having a stimulating moment with Jesus. I was praying up a storm. That is when I caught the eye of the person stopped next to me at the red light. They looked petrified, and when the light changed, they made haste to put distance between our two cars. I am sure they thought I needed help – and I did. Practicing, visualizing, entertaining the Presence of God enriches prayer. A few moments of very real focus makes His Presence more palpable throughout the day.

4. Keep Your Poise. With joy and peace on either side, coupled with a sense of His Presence, we are called to keep our poise – moderation, balance, gentleness, graciousness, and let that quality of life be made known to all men. Notice the three things that stand together here: joy, grace (poise and balance), and peace. Our nose is up. We are poised under pressure. We are making happy sounds. These are the veritable marks of a true believer.

This is the evidentiary proof of transformation that we are to offer as a witness to a watching world. "Having done all to stand, stand" in peace! Stay on your feet. Travel light. Let go of the hurts that have strings attached to them, that manipulate and draw you back to some unproductive place in your past. Forgive, not because the act was just or the person committing it has recognized the wrong and offered reconciliation. Do it for exactly the opposite reason. Do it to detach from the poison contained in the encounter. Remember, He who angers you, controls you! God should be the only one who can "push our buttons" and evoke behavior.

So Jesus would urge, *"If someone smites you on the right cheek, turn to him the other!"* (Matthew 5:39) He is not calling us to concede to abuse or celebrate it, but to be free from it. To be so poised that we choose, under direct personal attack, to act, and not react. Our poise is intact. We were created in the image of God, and then recreated, through the new birth, to be formed into the image of Christ. Were we to smite back, we would only allow ourselves to be made, if only for a moment, in the image of an angry aggressor. The Evil One would have succeeded in pulling us into his orbit. He would have again pressed his behavioral image onto our fleshly response. Jesus is urging us to have the moral capacity for differentiation from the world and the devil – to act and not react.

5. Refuse to Worry. We are implored – "Don't worry!" A prohibition is never effective alone. So three positive actions are commanded. First, *pray!* The word here is one for worship. Actually, it is a word indicating our orientation. Plainly, Paul is exhorting us to get our eyes off the problem and face heaven. Get a good look at God! See the solution, not the enemy. Gaze at the empty cross and the tomb. *"He is not here. He is risen!"*

Conrad Hilton, who built one of the world's great hotel chains noted, "Success seems to be connected with action. Successful people keep moving. They make mistakes, but they don't quit."

6. Worship. The word carries the idea of "facing God." When God breathed into Adam's nostrils, and dead clay came to life and Adam opened his eyes for the first time – God was in his face.[2] His trouble came when he allowed himself to gaze on the forbidden. Turn your face toward God. Gaze on Him. He is the One to whom you are appealing. The atmosphere of a prayer request demands worship. Be flexible and open to His will. And finally, be grateful.

Everything in the passage seems incongruent with normal human behavior. A needy state coupled with joy, peace, poise, worship and gratitude. Specifically, the need, whatever it is, when presented to God, is to be paired with some previous request that was granted. Here again, it is our focus being challenged. Fixated on the pulsating moment, the pain, the deficit, the loss, we are likely to be overwhelmed and plunged into despair. But, by deliberately partnering the need with some past trial for which there was an answer, we have hope. And hope empowers faith!

7. Be Flexible. Second, after worship, we "petition" God, but the word here is unique. It indicates the need to pray in a pliable, flexible way. *Supplication* means to bend before God in prayer. It may also mean that we are to be bendable in His hand, flexible, open to options, not fixed and rigid, not fragile and breakable, not forcing our will on God, but searching for His will in any matter. Jesus first asked for an exception, *"Let this cup pass!"* But He was bendable in the hands of the Father, *"Nevertheless, not My will but Thine be done!"* If it is not possible, He concedes, aligning His will with that of the Father (Luke 22:42).

Rejoice. Let peace stand guard. Maintain your balance. Remain cognizant of the Presence of the Lord. Whatever needs you have – offer them to God. Be flexible as you pray (supplication), be grateful, expressing your thanks with your petitions. Don't worry – worship. Turn your face in a worshipful gaze of God. Then handing your problems off to God, and expecting his intervention, be flexible, supple in his hand. Pour your soul out to him. Weep. Cry. And then face the world with the confidence, that he hears your prayers and will answer.

Max Lucado says,

If God had a refrigerator, your picture would be on it. If he had a wallet, your photo would be in it. He sends flowers every spring, a sunrise every morning. Whenever you want to talk, he will listen. He could live anywhere in the universe, but he chose your heart. What about the Christmas gift He sent you in Bethlehem, not to mention that Friday at Calvary Face it, He's crazy about you.[3]

8. Be Thankful and Grateful. Third, after worship and noting your need before God in a 'supple' manner, review His record with you, breakthroughs in the past, and offer gratitude. And then make a request that He intervene and meet the need. Tell God your problems, detail the requests, but then partner the petition with thanksgiving. Don't worry. Instead – pray in a thankful, worshipful and confident way. There is an old rhyme burned into my heart, the author long forgotten. "I had the blues, because I had no shoes; until upon the street, I met a man with no feet."

I recently arrived in Rome for an overnight on my way to Africa. I had been on the road for five days and had another week before I returned home. I had reserved a room at the airport for convenience and I was looking forward to a good night of sleep in preparation for a long, tiring flight from Europe to Zambia the next day. In Rome, I discovered that my bag was still in Germany. Wonderful.

The off-brand airline on which I flew did not have a convenient baggage office. I scrambled to find someone who could speak English. "You meana' – you looka for your bag, No?" The directions that followed sent me from one end of Terminal One to the far end of Terminal Three. "O, No! You no wanta be here. You wanta go backa to Terminal Two. Ana bagga services, Yes?" Back to Terminal Two. I looked everywhere. Ah, the sign said, 'Informacion!' A kind lady pointed me toward a flight of stairs. Upward I bounded on weary feet. But there was no baggage counter to be found. More advice. "O, no sir," the ticket agent told me with a frown, "You have make bigga' mistake. You musta claima your bagga before you exit security. Herea, I givea you a note. And I drawa you a mapa."

I needed a map. I was readmitted through security – still trying to read foreign signs with a dab of English here and there, but there was still no baggage claim office. But there was the polizia – my seventh attempt at sound advice or clear understanding, the fault being mine. I had already considered simply laying down and acting dead. "Follow him! He will lead you there," the officer declared authoritatively. A young Italian pushing a luggage cart turned and caught the eyes of the officer and of mine. "He willa followa you. You takea him to the baggage office." I felt like climbing on the baggage cart, but the young Italian was faster than my weary feet. I followed at a distance, with the gap between us increasing. Occasionally, he turned to see if I was still in tow.

I reached the counter only to find a long line. I was last. I waited, filed my claim, asked if they could forward my bag to Africa, picked up a toothbrush and headed to the Hilton, two-and-a-half hours after I had hoped to be there. It was now after 11:00 PM, and the connecting bridge from the airport to the hotel had been closed. Another officer. "You will have to go to the next terminal. Go down to ground level. Go outside. Go to Terminal One. Then go upstairs, and you can go across on that bridge, and then turn back…just follow the signs."

Exactly. That's what I had been doing for hours, it seemed. He was right. That bridge was open. I crossed it, and another covered walkway brought me back to the place where the bridge from Terminal Two would have taken me. Barbara had been praying that I would exercise more. Her prayer was being answered. She and God have a kind of conspiracy against me. The Hilton was still a good long distance away – probably half a mile. I walked, and when I could, I used the moving belt taking me through a maze of parking garages. I was sure I had gone too far, when I saw the end of the tunnel and no Hilton. In fact, I began to encounter homeless people, bedding down for the night on either side of me. Some were already soundly asleep. One lay clutching a plastic bag, probably filled with all his earthly possessions. Another was laying next to a luggage cart with a cardboard box on it. A drape over it provided a kind of tent. Some had thin blankets. Others seemed prepared to sleep on the bare concrete or lean against the wall of the corridor. Several were stirring about. Suddenly, my lost bag in this sea of homeless folks, my frustrating episode in trying to file a lost baggage claim, seemed less significant. At last, I saw the sign for the Hilton. Down the stairs I went again, following an outside walkway. Into the plush hotel I bounded, a world away from the homeless a few yards removed. Even without a suitcase with fresh clothes, there would be a warm shower. The room was luscious. The bed was soft. The climate was cool. The space was safe. What did I really have to complain about? Wading through the small faction of homeless people had put everything into perspective. I had so many reasons to be grateful.

9. Check Out the Jurors. Have you ever been disqualified for service on a jury? Maybe you have been a victim of a crime, and the attorney for the defense is concerned that you will transfer your feelings from your experience and penalize his client – so he moves for your dismissal.

Qualifying the jurors is a key part of the courtroom process. Today, in some cases, jurors are scrutinized as much as evidence. Get the wrong juror, and you end up with a hung jury. You lose your case. You need to check out the inner jurors…

10. Make the Exchange. This is not heaven – this is an earth so full of pain that at times it is hellish. What do we do with all these assaults on our senses? How do we handle life's pressures? We trade them, unload them, and cast them on the Lord – in order to maintain our balance. This is not a call to irresponsibility. It is not permission to disconnect from life and adopt a Pollyanna world view. The trade of our problems for graceful poise is accomplished in prayer – passionate prayer. When Jesus was arrested and faced the cross, when He was led through the mockery of a trial, He stood erect, and acted as the manly King that He was!

But, a few hours before, He had fallen under the weight of the crushing reality of His last hour. He had poured out His soul to the Father. He had sweat great drops of blood. He had confided to His disciples, *"My heart is nearly breaking within Me!"* (Mark 14:33) The Greek word is highly descriptive – *ekthambeó* (ek-tham-beh'-o). It means to be "to be thrown into a terror!" This is a rare view of Jesus, a fragile moment of vulnerability in which He asked the Father, *"If it be possible, let this cup pass!"* It is only seen in the context of prayer. In prayer, there is a place for weakness and tears, vulnerability and utter transparency.

We hemorrhage before the wrong audience. We ask men to do for us what only God can do. Jesus, in prayer, reconciles Himself to the will of His Father, and nobly faces the cross. He places Himself and His plight, His circumstances and His enemies, into the hand of the Father. His mission now is not to remove the pain or escape the cross, but to carry Himself in such a way that He does not in His final hours sin, miss the mark, behave in a belligerent or vengeful way and end up trapped under the line of sin and death, as did the first Adam.

This is a moment that demanded ultimate balance. He must not only carry Himself, He must also carry the sins of the world. The hate around Him cannot be allowed to infect Him. He must act, not react. He must hold His tongue. He must retain presence of mind and poise! Having committed Himself, indeed, His life, to the Father, He will only concern Himself with the witness He offers the world in his final hours. He is certain that He will triumph. He assures others of a paradise that awaits. He is conscious of the world on top of this world. But Golgotha could only be endured because of grace for resolve and the power He found in Gethsemane, the garden of prayer!

A few years ago, God met me in this passage, Philippians 4:4-12. For weeks, it consumed me. It convicted me. It informed me. It challenged me to rethink prayer requests – to see that God was relieving me of earth's concerns so that I could focus on heaven's concern – being a joyful witness in the midst of trouble, remaining at peace even with multiple problems, keeping my poise under pressure – all by grace. There are, one scholar remarked, only two positions in prayer: petition and praise. Praise should be normative, but needs overwhelm us and repress praise. Petition engages God, to meet some need, "that I might praise," again. That is common in the psalms. But here, Paul pushes us to a new and higher standard, that we praise as we petition, before the answer comes. This is now the new New Testament normal. Joy, poise, peace.

Endnotes

1. Annie J. Flint, "He Giveth More Grace" (Copyright: Public Domain; Orchard Park, New York: First released in the "Casterline Card" Series). library.timelesstruths.org/music/He_Giveth_More_Grace/
2. Idea from a sermon preached by Pastor Mike Cowart in Heidelberg, Germany, the 2011 Servicemen's Center Leader Retreat.
3. Max Lucado, *The Lucado Life Lessons Study Bible,* 83.

THE GREAT EXCHANGE

Why Your Prayer Requests May Not Be Getting Answers

RESOURCE KIT

Includes:

- Book
- Personal Study Guide with Group It
- Flash Drive with Teaching Guide, PowerPoint file and video sessions

Use as a resource for personal growth or as a small group for discipleship study. Includes 12 sessions with support materials.

www.alivepublications.org